Mastering Ministry's Pressure Points

WHO'S IN CHARGE?

Standing Up to Leadership Pressures

LEITH ANDERSON
JACK HAYFORD
BEN PATTERSON

MULTNOMAH BOOKS

WHO'S IN CHARGE?
© 1993 by Christianity Today, Inc.

Published by Multnomah Press Books
Questar Publishers, Inc.
Sisters, Oregon

Printed in the United States of America

International Standard Book Number: 88070-541-8

Most Scripture quotations are from the *New International Version* (©1973, 1978, 1984
by the International Bible Society; used by permission of Zondervan Publishing House).

93 94 95 96 97 98 99 00 01 — 10 9 8 7 6 5 4 3 2 1

Contents

Introduction

Had the question come from a young pastor, I might have known how to respond. But the minister sitting across the chrome and Formica table in the small-town cafe was no rookie.

"What should I be doing in my church?" he asked.

Conventional wisdom would have pointed him to preaching, prayer, and pastoral care. But he was already doing such things. His struggle lay deeper: not how to perform ministry skills but in what direction to point them.

"I'm not a visionary, not a type-A personality," he explained. "I don't have grand ambitions or the inner drive to stretch people to accomplish great things. I'm a pastor. I enjoy talking with people about God, Scripture, life, death, their families, and their character."

The previous pastor had been forced out by the congregation a few years earlier, and the people had been wary, slow to warm up to the new minister. But over three years, Jerry had won their respect and even their affection. From my conversations with members of his church, I knew he had become their pastor.

"He's real," said one.

"We can tell he loves us," said another.

So what was Jerry's frustration?

"I feel like I should be doing something more," he said. "But what exactly? Where should I put my efforts?"

He was feeling one of the pressures of leadership: to make fruitful use of one's time and gifts, especially to know the best thing to do next. Leaders want to hear, "Well done, good and faithful servant." But they often struggle to define what is good and faithful in their unique setting.

We talked about what made his church unique and how other pastors used their time: one pastor, for instance, upon coming to a new and troubled church, spent the first year healing strained relationships, the next year developing the infrastructure (primarily small groups and the youth program), and year three reaching out to the community.

We also talked about how Jerry felt he might spend his time for the coming year, but we reached no firm conclusions. I came away, though, with a new appreciation for Jerry and for pastors who are sometimes confused as to what it means to be the leader.

Leadership demands casting vision and setting up structures and making decisions and motivating volunteers. It means upholding standards, resisting temptation to take the easy way out, deciding what to say when to whom. A leader has to be organized and creative, patient and efficient. Leaders have to work with people who drain them physically, mentally, emotionally, and spiritually.

In our work with LEADERSHIP, the practical journal for pastors, the other editors and I have met countless pastors who admit to feeling overwhelmed by their responsibilities. This book, along with the others in this series, focuses on how to handle the pressure points of ministry. It's written by three men who have proven their ability to minister effectively under pressure.

Leith Anderson

Leith Anderson is not afraid of change — to say the least.

Since 1977, Leith has served as senior pastor of Wooddale Church in Eden Prairie, a suburb of Minneapolis. His tenure there hasn't been quiet. Under his leadership, the church relocated, changed its official name (from Wooddale Baptist Church), expanded its facilities, planted a daughter congregation, and developed a reputation for innovative and well-targeted ministries. In the process, membership has doubled.

Such massive changes do not happen automatically, and certainly not without pressure on the leader. Many of these pressures are reflected in Leith's chapters in this book.

Leith is not only a strong leader, he is a student of the art of leadership and of contemporary culture. His recent books, *Dying for Change* and *A Church for the 21st Century* and *Mastering Church Management* (Multnomah), demonstrate Leith's ability to understand a changing society, diagnose the church's situation, and point the way to effective ministry. He's also a LEADERSHIP contributing editor.

He pursued his education at Moody Bible Institute, Bradley University, and Denver Seminary, and he has a doctor of ministry degree from Fuller Theological Seminary. Ten years at Calvary Baptist Church in Longmont, Colorado, gave Leith his early ministry experience, and today he's in demand as a speaker, seminar leader, and seminary educator.

In this volume, Leith turns his attention from meeting the challenges the outside world brings to handling the weight of the interior world of the leader.

Jack Hayford

In 1969 Jack Hayford began a "temporary assignment" to pastor eighteen people at Church on the Way, in Van Nuys, California. Today nearly ten thousand attend weekly services.

Jack is not only the leader of this church, he is a leader within the charismatic movement, he helps lead an interdenominational fellowship of pastors in the Los Angeles area, and he's recognized as a worship leader whose songs (including the hymn "Majesty") have been widely used in congregational singing.

After graduating from LIFE Bible College in Los Angeles, he took a pastorate in Fort Wayne, Indiana. He returned to Los Angeles to serve as national youth director for the International Church of the Foursquare Gospel and then became a professor at LIFE before going to Church on the Way.

He has written several books, including *Worship His Majesty*, *Rebuilding the Real You*, and *Mastering Worship* (Multnomah).

As you will see in this book, Jack has faced some ulcer-causing dilemmas, and he's handled them with grace, wisdom, and poise. His approach is one from which others in ministry can benefit.

Ben Patterson

Ben Patterson's ministry has taken him from coast to coast, and he's traveled even farther culturally. He went from a mildly counter-cultural church he planted in the suburban sprawl of Orange County, California, to a small, woodsy New Jersey town, to pastor a congregation with two hundred years of tradition and a cemetery surrounding the white, steepled building.

And, like countless pastors, he's straddled the even wider differences found among the diverse individuals who inhabit a single congregation.

Ben thrives on such diversity. He still sports a beard and wears an open collar and sweater to the office — even though his New Providence Presbyterian Church (in the town of the same name) is church home for many who commute to Wall Street or the headquarters of IBM or AT&T.

In addition to pastoring, Ben hosts a radio program and is a contributing editor to CHRISTIANITY TODAY and LEADERSHIP. He is author of *Waiting: Finding Hope When God Seems Silent* and *Mastering the Pastoral Role* (Multnomah).

Ben is direct, honest, sometimes brash. At the same time, he's disarming in his willingness to acknowledge the pressures of ministry and how he handles them — or fails to handle them as he'd like. His candor and his competence both clearly emerge.

The Pressure Cooker

Mark Twain once noted that "War talk by men who have been in a war is always interesting; whereas moon talk by a poet who has not been on the moon is likely to be dull." This book is war talk of sorts. It's been written by individuals who are still on the front lines.

In addition to the three authors, I want to commend three others who helped create this book and the subsequent volumes in this series: Mark Galli, Brian Larson, and David Goetz, the editors of this book series. They worked closely with the authors, interviewing them, editing the transcripts, and talking again with the authors to make the contents both practical and pleasant to read.

I trust you'll find, as I did, that while church leadership has its pressure points, the three authors of this book provide wisdom and strength to stand up to the task.

These are their stories and their insights.

— *Marshall Shelley*
Editor, LEADERSHIP

Part 1
The Leader's Role

———————————————

The pastor, as a visionary, is like an architect who intimately knows each room in the building he or she is designing long before it's actually constructed.

— Leith Anderson

I'm the Leader — Now What?

I_t was May of 1969. I had just crammed three years of seminary into two and couldn't wait to reap the rewards of surviving my education: full-time ministry. The church I had been serving part time asked me to become their associate pastor. Charleen and I were ecstatic.

By the end of that summer, the senior pastor had resigned, and I was named his successor. At age 24, I was handed the reins of a local church.

Most of my training prepared me for the one hour on Sunday

morning. The first few months, I studied and planned until lunch. After lunch I headed for home. With my parishioners working during the day, I had nobody to visit, so at first I took afternoon naps or caught up on the afternoon soap operas! I returned to work in the evenings, visiting or attending church meetings.

A lot has changed since then — I now work afternoons. But regularly I'm faced with the same question: as a leader, exactly what am I supposed to do? This is especially true the first days of a new pastorate (or during the transition into a new chapter of church life). What should I do with my time? Where exactly should I lead the church? And what are the first steps I should take to lead them into the future, whatever that might be?

Recognize Your Swirling Emotions

I enjoyed baseball as a boy. Once while playing catcher, I stood up to grab a wild pitch. As I stretched for the ball, the batter swung, hitting me on the back of my head and laying me out across home plate. After that, I became a reluctant catcher.

Pastors can also feel reluctant to stretch for a new direction, fearful of risking their neck in the process. Many emotions swirl within us as we begin a new ministry. These emotions are neither good nor bad. But we are wise to monitor them so they don't undermine our work.

We may begin to wonder, for instance, if we're using our time wisely. I felt guilty for not working afternoons during the early days of my first pastorate, even though I studied at the office until noon and attended church meetings in the evenings. It never dawned on me that I didn't have to work from 7:00 A.M. to 11:00 P.M.

We are wise to be aware of the emotional tug to be busy, making sure our emotions don't pressure us into patterns of ministry that will raise false expectations. Some pastors, especially in smaller communities, feel the pull to visit every family in their congregation the first year. This can have enormous value for pastors' immediate credibility, but it also raises expectations that can destroy them later.

People will expect to be visited regularly and have a special friendship with the pastor. When that doesn't happen — and it can't over the long haul — pockets of dissension about not being nurtured surface. Relationships with members, important though they may be, can consume an inordinate amount of our energies. That can undermine our ability to lead the church effectively.

I wound up filling many afternoons by reading biographies of famous Christians such as Robert Murray McCheyne, Charles Haddon Spurgeon, and David Brainerd. I gleaned much from the trials and successes of these great people.

Another powerful emotion is the desire to be accepted by the members. When Patti Hearst, the daughter of a wealthy California family, was kidnapped in the 1970s by the Symbionese Liberation Army and held for ransom, no one suspected she would surface with a submachine gun, robbing Northern California banks alongside her captors. Through her long ordeal, she was sucked into acting like her captors. She became one of them.

The Patti Hearst syndrome can also affect pastors. Wanting to be accepted and liked by our congregations, we can become too much like those we're trying to lead.

One Saturday morning, while standing in my Colorado church parking lot, a man walked up to me and handed me the church constitution. Pointing to the section on the pastor's responsibilities, he highlighted my duty to do pastoral care.

"I think you're neglecting the elderly in our church," he said. What he really meant was "I want my own elderly parents to be visited more."

"Visitation is only one of my many duties, Bob," I replied, "and I believe the bases are being covered." I, too, felt pastoral care was important, but I refused to let it become the driving force of my ministry — it isn't what I'd been called to emphasize.

I also felt the pressure to offer altar calls at the end of each church service. But I believed it to be counterproductive to evangelism, making it harder for the people in our community to believe.

I wanted to be liked, but I resisted the temptation to blend in with their way of doing things just to please them.

A third strong emotion is our eagerness to succeed. I am the son of a successful pastor. Thirty years ago, few Protestant congregations could boast a thousand Sunday morning worshipers. The church my father pastored, located near New York City, could. The church bore many of the external trappings of success, including a multiple staff and a large budget. This became to me an unwritten standard of success.

Financial considerations intensify this pressure to be successful. When Charleen and I left seminary, we needed a washer and dryer, so we drove to Sears and charged them. We also needed a new car, so we obligated ourselves to car payments for three years. In short, I couldn't afford to lose my job.

Tangled up in the emotions of wanting to succeed is the fear of failure. I still feel this fear. I sometimes wonder if a reason I'm still at Wooddale is my fear of not being able to repeat success in another church. Ultimately, I'm convinced Wooddale is where God has called me, and frankly I'm excited at what God is doing in the church. But periodically, a quiet fear of failure lets itself be known.

Finally, there is the fear of inadequacy. Even though I had grown up in a parsonage, I wasn't prepared for the emotions that stirred within me when I dealt with people's problems. When I was a young pastor, a woman came to see me about her difficult marriage. In addition to her marital struggles, she had physical and financial problems. Her list of maladies was endless. I helped her as best I could. I prayed with her and even called a local physician, making an appointment for her.

One afternoon after hearing about her tragic life again, I drove home, laid down on my bed, and wept. I felt so inadequate to deal with her problems.

Entering a new phase of ministry can raise latent fears about our capabilities. When we've admitted these emotions, we're ready to tackle the tasks of leadership.

Do First Things First

When entering a new ministry, we've got to do some things, and that means not doing other things. But of the multitude of possibilities that exist, what are the essentials, the wisest investments that will yield the greatest return?

First, I do the things that the church culture demands.

A pediatrician in our church completed a short-term mission service in Africa. She was the only physician on duty in the African hospital where she worked. On one occasion, she admitted a woman who couldn't deliver a baby and needed a Caesarean section. Though the pediatrician wasn't skilled in delivering babies, much less by Caesarean section, she performed the operation, saving the lives of both the mother and child. The doctor did what she had to do.

The same holds true for pastors. There are certain things that pastors must do — whether we are experts at it or not, and whether or not we like it.

Some pastors might say, "I'm not a morning person." But if they are ministering in communities where people rise early for work, they too must turn on their office lights at 8:00 A.M. Otherwise, they will be perceived as lazy, even if they work late into the evenings. The church culture demands that only after their credibility as hard workers has been established can they revert to their preferred routine.

When I became a full-time pastor, I recognized that something needed to be done about evangelism. Although my father was a pastor and I a seminary graduate, I didn't know much about evangelism. So I started reading books on the subject until I thought I had the principles down pat. One of the principles was training lay people. So I found a lay person, dragged him with me for my first evangelism visit, and made a complete fool of myself.

Evangelism wasn't — and still isn't — my gift. But it needed to be done. The context dictated that I begin a program, even if evangelism wasn't maximizing my own personal giftedness.

Doing what has to be done initially runs counter with today's emphasis of focusing on one's gifts. I also subscribe to Peter Drucker's principle of going with our strengths, not our weaknesses. Beginning a new chapter of ministry, though, requires us to do what needs to be done, priming the engine and then fueling it later with someone who is gifted and much better at it than we are.

We must resist the temptation to build a twenty-year strategy based on our weaknesses. Still, we must be driven by mission and purpose rather than personality.

Second, I try to get some successes under my belt. Success will give us credibility we'll need later.

One way to success is by visiting revered, elderly people in the congregation. Another may be to ask a beloved predecessor to speak some Sunday, validating the church tradition that preceded you.

Planning and executing church programs with a high probability of success is also important. The first full summer of full-time pastoring, I proposed a four-week series of evening films called "August in the Park." We gathered at sunset in a nearby city park and showed Christian films on a large screen. Hundreds came from the church and community. The effort multiplied Sunday evening church attendance, communicated we were interested in outreach, made parishioners feel good about their church, and bolstered my pastoral credibility. Everyone was a winner.

Preparing for the Long Haul

As I take care of these two essentials, I'm already beginning to think how I want to lead for the next few years. That to me is what it means to be a leader on day one, day two, and the rest of my ministry at that church.

To lead, the pastor must create vision for the local church. A vision has to start with someone, and that someone often is the pastor. Years ago, when Wooddale relocated to our present facility, no one believed it could be done. As a leader of Wooddale, I was responsible to voice the vision to build a facility.

Someone with vision lives in the future. I "lived" in our new facility at Wooddale for years before the church actually moved in. The pastor, as a visionary, is like an architect who intimately knows each room in the building he or she is designing long before it's actually constructed.

Though the pastor takes initiative, the vision is honed and

developed by others. The others may be staff members or lay leaders who are more gifted and talented, who make real the dream God has given, giving it sophistication, expanding and developing it in ways he or she never could.

Tailoring the Dream

A visionary pastor faces a big challenge: creating a dream that is rooted in the timeless truth of Scripture and then tailoring it to reach the local community for Christ. Here is a framework to begin:

● *Develop a theology of ministry.* My basis for local church vision is grounded in the birth of Christ. By invading time, the Son of God risked all, inaugurating the recovery of paradise lost by coming to do the work of the Father. Christ is our model, the prototype for taking risks and planning to reach our community to do God's work in our locale.

This transcends New Jersey, Minnesota, or California. The vision for a Colorado community, corralled by sugar beet fields and cattle, will look different than in Minneapolis, which is inhabited by universities, corporations, and hospitals. But the underlying theology is the same: to do the work of the Father.

● *Discover the church's values.* In addition to rooting our vision theologically, we also must understand the community where we live. The pastor must function like a physician diagnosing a patient's condition. Often that requires digging into the past.

One of the first things I did in Colorado was to read the minutes of the various boards and committees for the entire history of the church. I also visited families in the congregation to hear their perceptions about the church. Such research pays rich dividends.

Recently I talked to a pastor who ministers in a 140-year-old congregation. Flipping through the church's minutes from over a hundred years ago, he discovered that the last names of those making and seconding the motions were often identical to those making and seconding motions on his present board. The grandparents and great-grandparents of his congregation dealt with the same issues the same way their children were dealing with them. The church's problems, he realized, had less to do with the issues and more to do with the families who dominated the church.

Discovering the values of a local church is usually learned the hard way: experience. Wooddale's previous pastor was a gifted musician who led the church successfully for nineteen years. I, on the other hand, took piano lessons for eight years as a child but never finished the second lesson book. So when I arrived at Wooddale, I couldn't match my predecessor in many areas. Even though I had carefully researched my compatibility with Wooddale, I endured criticism for my inabilities.

• *Become an ethnologist.* Several years ago, a California church pursued me to be their senior pastor. I discovered later that they had hired an FBI-type person to research me. I also was surprised to find out that he knew so much about me. That church was committed to matching someone to their specific culture.

I had this same commitment coming to Wooddale — only I did a background check on a church, not an individual. In a library, I scanned the history of Minneapolis. I familiarized myself with the local schools as well as the local economy.

I also found another candidate whom Wooddale had previously interviewed, and I talked with him at length, asking for details of his interview. Before I ever agreed to a first interview, I had a general picture of the church and the community in which it was located.

• *Begin studying the local culture.* While construction was underway for our worship center at Wooddale, a church consultant, leading a group from his local seminar, walked through our partially completed building and remarked, "Here is a good example of how not to build a church. It looks like a church — a turn off to today's generation."

He assumed what worked in Southern California would work in Minneapolis, Minnesota. In our research, though, we discovered that people in our culture wanted a church to look like a church, a value embedded in the heritage of the community.

As a new pastor I studied and analyzed the local culture immediately. During the candidating process, this cannot be done in depth. But it is essential in the early phase of a new ministry. We cannot discover the church's priorities without understanding the culture in which we minister.

● *Put it all together.* As I think about my theology of ministry, the church's values, and the culture of the community, I ask myself: what would the church look like if these three elements were combined?

The vision for a church includes imaginary people (who they are and how they relate to each other), imaginary programs that touch the community with the gospel, and imaginary facilities that allow the ministry of the gospel to penetrate the local culture. Long before we relocated and became a church that reaches out, we "saw" ourselves reaching new people through a new program of support groups. To some it was an idea on a list. To those of us with the vision, we could almost see the faces, hear the voices, see people pull up chairs in a room.

Investing in Momentum

Actually, putting those three ingredients together doesn't solve my problems. It probably produces more ideas than can be possibly accomplished in a three-, five-, or even ten-year plan. Next is to decide which idea should be tackled first.

● *Go with your strengths.* According to Peter Drucker, organizations, like individual leaders, should focus on their strengths.

Too often, churches invest heavily in weak programs, never developing the momentum needed for growth. If a church is strong in worship and weak in Sunday school, the worship must be promoted and expanded first. Later the Sunday school can be created, fed by the resources of a healthy worship service.

Not long after I arrived at Wooddale, we inaugurated a small-group ministry and various social activities, emphasizing our strength in fellowship. Our people were good at relationships, and so focusing on their gifts became an effective means of incorporating new people.

Often right choices run counter to peer pressure. Designated gifts to bolster weak areas, for example, can undermine this strategy. It's tempting to accept the gift. But just because someone donates $1,000 for refurbishing Sunday school rooms doesn't mean the church should make plans for renovation.

● *Find the quickest return.* One year we faced the important decision of whom to add to the staff. One faction in the church lobbied heavily for a counseling pastor.

But our counseling program was weak. Our singles ministry, however, was already up and running. In addition, the metropolitan area provided many resources for Christian counseling, but a largely unreached singles population existed in our community. So we went with a singles pastor. As a result, our singles ministry exploded, reaching many unchurched singles in the community and adding excitement to a growing congregation.

In American culture, most suburban and urban churches need a critical mass of people to develop growth momentum. To reach that critical mass, which hovers near three hundred worshipers in most suburban settings, pastors must invest in programs with quick returns, targeting ministries with high impact and immediate results. Churches today need an irreducible minimum of resources — people and money — to attract newcomers. Basic programs like children and youth ministries are needed to draw the people that will enable the church to grow.

Shifting Gears

Creating a local church vision is one thing. Implementing that vision is another. Small churches function on a hub-and-spoke model of operation. The pastor is the hub, and the church members are the spokes, relating directly to the pastor.

One frazzled pastor was at the end of his rope. He had led his church to exciting new growth — 700 attenders filled the sanctuary on Sunday mornings — but now he couldn't keep up the pace. During our long conversation, he complained about his unmotivated congregation and the problems on his elder board.

"There's nothing wrong with your church," I said, when I finally got a word in. "The best solution may be for you to leave, to hand the reins of leadership to someone who can lead a church of that size."

As his church grew, I discovered, this pastor wasn't able to change his leadership style. He started working harder, still trying to operate on the hub-and-spoke model. He ended up logging eighty-hour workweeks.

When I pastored a small church, I frequently stopped by the hospital on my way home from work, just in case someone I knew was there. When a baby arrived, I was the first to know, even if it was 2:00 A.M. "It's a girl" or "It's a boy," I'd often hear as I'd pick up the phone in the middle of the night.

Few call me today. I had to relinquish close relationships with a majority of the congregation so that their needs could be met by someone else and the kingdom of God expanded. I had to move from being the hub of the wheel to being the axle, moving from a direct to a more indirect relationship to the congregation. New systems of leadership had to be developed, distributing relationships and power to other pastors and leaders in the church.

Risking the Ship

In 1990, when Wooddale was building its worship center, I was convinced we should be planting churches to reach the community for Christ. If we were serious about evangelism, then we needed to grow new churches, one of the most effective means of evangelism. A church building was merely a means to an end, not the end itself.

Some thought me crazy. They argued that we'd be committing financial suicide by planting a church in the middle of a building project — we needed all the money and bodies we could muster.

"Wait until we have more people," I heard over and over again. "Plant a church after we move into our new worship center."

By planting a new congregation, I felt we were making a powerful statement about our purpose: we were willing to risk crippling a major church project to reach people for Christ. The leadership got on board, and finally the congregation voted to plant the church, which in the end, didn't sabotage our building project.

Recently, while sitting on an airplane, I glanced at the aeronautics magazine the passenger next to me was reading. A picture of a Boeing 777 accompanied the article. The headline read, "Boeing Risks the Company Again."

I discovered Boeing had risked the company in 1957 when it unveiled the first commercial jet aircraft — the 707. Boeing gambled again in the late sixties by producing the first wide-body plane — the 747. Now they were planning to do it again with the 777.

I realize there will never be a time when I'm not carrying out these principles. While these issues are most acute in a new situation, new situations never really go away. Pastors who lead effectively must be willing to risk the ship repeatedly for the sake of the gospel. In one sense, we'll never stop asking, "I'm the leader — now what?"

I want to be a warm and gentle pastor who comforts and the visionary leader who challenges.

— *Jack Hayford*

CHAPTER TWO

How to Lead *and* Feed

One Saturday years ago some stunning, painful news came to me. Through a counseling conversation, I discovered that a pastor in our church had fallen into adultery. Since I trusted the person giving me this information, I knew I had to act — but what should I do exactly? I didn't want to presume his guilt; then again, if he was at fault, I had to deal with him.

The following Tuesday, that same pastor snapped at another staff member, so I decided to call him into my office to talk about that. Meanwhile, I hoped he would acknowledge his immorality in the course of the conversation.

Having known and even been involved in the training of this young man for years, I could be direct. In fact, I was pretty hard on him about his snapping remark. "We don't treat each other like that," I stressed. Then, spontaneously, I added, "But that's not the only problem here, is it?"

He looked up at me, began to tremble, hung his head, and wept.

I wept with him. He was not an evil man, but he had succumbed to weakness.

In the days that followed, I walked a fine line. I needed to lead, to take a strong stand against sexual sin, both with this man in private and before the entire church. Yet I needed to be pastoral, bringing healing and restoration. Both were essential for this individual and his wife, as well as the church.

This is just one example of the tension between leading and feeding. And it is a tension.

When a pastor primarily feeds, people enjoy the church but lack a corporate sense of destiny. They graze comfortably in the valley and never climb to new heights. The church has a warm, fuzzy feeling, and people enjoy the inspiration and fellowship, but they're not trying to achieve anything. Sheep don't want to climb mountains. They're happy as long as they have a patch of grass.

If a pastor emphasizes leading, on the other hand, he or she may drive the sheep into the ground, pushing them up the mountain without allowing them to stop and eat. If the flock makes it to the top, they're dizzy with weariness, and the burnout quotient increases.

I want to be the warm and gentle pastor who comforts *and* the visionary leader who challenges. I've found, although difficult at times, it's possible to do both.

The Difficulties

In some ways, leading and feeding can complement one another. But we should be aware of the special problems and difficulties that arise as we try to do both. Here are a few issues that challenge me.

1. *Difficult people.* Some people are parasites. Often something terrible happened in their past, and no matter how much attention you give them, they want more, personally, from you alone. When they touch you, you can feel the energy drain right out of you.

In dealing with such people, I am torn between caring for them and attending to the leadership tasks that benefit the entire church. I seek to show warmth and acceptance, while others with a gift for merciful ministry give greater, sustained attention to these needy, draining types.

As these individuals call the weaker person to Christian growth and discipline, I buttress their demands and declared expectations. So I'm more than just "a nice guy." My acceptance lays a foundation for the effective ministry of mercy by others — and the tension between leading (calling to growth) and feeding (patient nurturing) is maintained.

2. *Misunderstandings.* When dealing with issues such as personal evangelism, faith promises for missions, tithing, or personal devotions, I cringe at the misconceptions people have. Many of their false assumptions can too easily cause misunderstandings. For instance, in each of our church services, we have twenty to forty visitors who, when I talk about money, could immediately assume, *That's what I thought. They're after my money.*

So I'll often begin a discussion of money with a few qualifiers. "If you're attending our church for the first time, you need to know that I do not preach about money every week. It is an important subject for every Christian, and Jesus emphasized the impact that money has on our spiritual lives, but it is not the primary subject of the Bible or of my preaching. It just so happens that I'm talking about it today. My goal in preaching about money is to strengthen you, not to fill the church coffers."

I'm kidded in our congregation, in fact, for my lengthy preambles that try to defuse every possible objection before I get down to the business at hand. But I'm as anxious for people to know what I *don't* mean as what I do mean.

3. Challenging without condemning. The last thing I want to do is condemn people. But leadership means challenging people, pointing them to a higher plateau in Christ, sustaining a Philippians 3:13,14 "unsatisfied satisfaction." And the more concerned a pastor is with the deeper dimensions of Christian living — commitment, discipleship, purity of life, devotion to Christ, prayer — the easier it is to dump guilt or condemnation on the flock.

I reviewed the manuscript of another writer recently. He is a younger newcomer to ministry. I noticed that his style was condescending, calling others to growth with phrases such as "Shouldn't we as Christians do better than that?" and "You wouldn't want to fail the Lord, would you?" The article was negative, invoking a sense of failure rather than hope.

I encouraged him, "Turn those phrases around, so you don't invoke defeat or guilt but still call people to be responsible. That would sound something like this: 'With the Holy Spirit indwelling us, we need never fail our Lord Jesus. In him we can do all things!' "

How to Lead in a Way That Feeds

Shepherds lead sheep from pasture to pasture, and so for them, leading is inseparably linked with feeding. I find the same is true for me if I keep the following factors in mind.

● *Time the challenge.* In a Wednesday night service in 1973, a week before Thanksgiving, a man gave a prophetic exhortation about our congregation's future. We were to "intercede for America as if no one else were interceding." (Others were, of course, but we were to pray with a sense of urgency as though no one else was.) At the time, America was embroiled in Watergate and Viet Nam, and some journalists were wondering if America would reach its two-hundredth birthday.

I felt the prophetic word forcefully confirmed in my heart, but I didn't act on it immediately. I felt if we tried to launch a new prayer initiative in the middle of the holiday season, people would be too distracted to participate fully. I risked seeming forgetful of this word but felt the long-range call would be better served by a short-range waiting period.

The Lord confirmed my decision. I waited until after the New Year to follow through. The second Wednesday of January we began 7:14 prayer meetings (based on 2 Chronicles 7:14 — "If my people who are called by my name will humble themselves and pray . . ."). We gathered at 7:00, as usual, but at 7:14 each week we made extensive intercession for America.

Besides dynamic results in evidence as we prayed, further things happened. Eventually a music group from our church began traveling with the musical, "If My People," taking the call to prayer to sixty cities. We underwrote their quarter-million-dollar budget. Over the next two years, other intercessory projects branched off into radio and television, enlisting thousands of other intercessors.

Nineteen years later, we still offer the 7:14 prayers, but all of that might never have happened if we had tried to lead the people into something new at an unsuitable time.

● *Pace the challenge.* In a congregation of any size, only a percentage will respond immediately to a challenge. In a church of 150, if a pastor leads strongly on an issue, probably thirty at most will respond immediately and enthusiastically. Most will eventually follow, but it will take time.

People are in various degrees of spiritual health; they differ in their ability to hear, capacity to move, and willingness to follow. I can't lead at the pace of the fastest sheep in the flock, leaving behind the aged, the weak, or the sick. I'm obligated to lead the slower sheep as well. Congregations resembling elite Marine Corps units, which respond at a moment's notice, just don't exist. If I want to bring the maximum number of sheep with me, I must persuade even those who don't bound to their feet at my first call.

Church members won't follow if they doubt they can make it. Climbing into unknown territory is frightening. Although some followers can believe in the value of a leader's vision, they often don't believe they're good enough or spiritual enough to fulfill it. They doubt themselves more than they doubt their pastor's leadership or God's call.

So my leading and feeding will be to no avail unless I believe in my people. I have to believe they would fly if they could, that despite their weaknesses and faults, deep down inside they want to follow Christ. My people will believe in themselves if I lead at a pace they can handle. For example, I am sensitive to how many financial appeals we make per year and how often we ask people to cut extra time in their schedule for special church activities. When they can handle the schedule and their budget absorbs their sacrificial offerings, it gives them confidence.

They'll also believe in themselves if they are being fed. A healthy diet builds strength and brings confidence. Hunger brings a sense of defeat. If they feel defeated and hungry where they are, they'll never go farther.

Sheep follow if they know the shepherd invariably leads to more food. A feeding shepherd, because he or she gains their trust through his servant spirit, just has to give a verbal tug on the heart, and the people follow.

For instance, recently our church purchased a church building and grounds located about a half-mile from our current church. When the idea for this purchase first came to me, two years earlier, I knew it would be difficult for many in our church to accept: "How would we coordinate activities on two separate campuses?" they would rightfully ask. "How would parents drop off their kids in one building and attend church in another, blocks away?" I realized that I would need to prepare the people ahead of time before they could even consider the purchase.

I preached a series of sermons from the Book of Joshua on the subject of possessing the land. "God has a promise and a future for each of us, and for the church corporately, but we only receive it by going in and taking possession" was my repeated theme.

Months later, when I proposed buying the church to our leaders and eventually the congregation, the themes of Joshua formed the backdrop. The congregation later followed in this challenging venture because they had been adequately fed beforehand.

This to me is where the two aspects of pastoring come together: we can lead as we feed; we can feed as we lead.

• *Form enclaves for those who respond at a faster pace.* For the

"Marines" in our church, we provide settings where I can give a stronger challenge. I meet with one hundred young men each month to train them for leadership. I'm not gentle with them. I crowd in tight and hard in that meeting. I say things like "If you don't believe you're supposed to be serving this congregation, don't even come. Those who choose to attend here have made up their minds that we are followers of Jesus Christ. We're serious about prayer, we're in the Word, and we're committed to the church. We know that God wants us serving this particular church."

I'll talk in hard-nosed fashion about what kind of TV programs and movies the men watch, whether they laugh at the off-color jokes at work, how they manage their thought lives, especially their sexual imagination.

My leadership in this meeting isn't diplomatic or warm, but it is accepted because of the nature of the group.

I can also talk tough with these men because I'm tough on myself — transparent about my own life. I don't address subjects solely in terms of scriptural principles; I tell about my struggles and how I have dealt with them. I don't act as if I have accomplished perfection.

My transparency also cultivates hope among these future leaders. They seem to reason, *Jack means business. He's learned a path of fruitfulness with God, yet he also has struggles just like I do. So if he's struggled and overcome, then maybe I can overcome as well.*

● *Accept the inevitable losses.* In the army, when a leader makes a command decision that sends men into battle, he knows there will be casualties. Likewise I know that any church leader's decisions will result in some leaving — seeking a less demanding environment of commitment. I feel that loss deeply. I've never taken casually a person leaving the church. I want to think all our people will sooner or later follow my leadership, but that just isn't reality.

If members choose to leave our church, though, I've come to believe it's because I'm not their shepherd anymore. For whatever reason, they no longer hear the Great Shepherd's voice through me, so I must be content that God has another place for them.

In my early years of pastoral work, when anyone left the

church, it was terribly painful for me. Most likely, people left both because of my immaturity as a leader and because I served small and what were to some undesirable churches.

I know the temptation of struggling to retain people bent on leaving. I also know my personal blind-spots, my insensitivities that lead to "losing" people. I think I've overcome impersonal or insensitive ways and found a place of confidence in the Lord, so that if people are committed to leaving, I can "send them with blessing" rather than being pained or declaring them unreliable or disloyal.

● *Keep in step with the calendar.* Our church year begins in September. People return from vacations, and though busy, they are eager for new direction. My opportunity to lead them stretches from the second week in September until the middle of November. I project vision and deliver strength-building exposition at this time.

Holidays consume people's attention from Thanksgiving through the New Year; so I seek to inspire with truth relevant to the season's thrusts.

In January people are inclined to think about new goals and ambitions. That's when diet programs and exercise clubs advertise heavily. In January, I usually focus my preaching on discipleship themes, and in February we emphasize world missions.

Special opportunities come with the Lenten season, as people focus on what Christ has done for them on the cross and how they should respond. I usually preach on themes like redemption's perfect work, the promise in following Christ, and the person of Jesus.

There is a post-Easter letdown everywhere. I counter this with a strong emphasis in the weeks leading up to Pentecost. Spirit-filled living and resurrection power for service are themes here. We also make a strong emphasis on family and marriage at this time.

In early June we prepare for summer. Even though everyone will be going their separate ways, we find a way to focus on something together, usually by asking everyone to read the same book, devotionally follow the same Bible readings, and memorize the same Scriptures.

● *Be aware of people's concerns.* In January of 1991 I interrupted our church plans because of the Persian Gulf War. Many had family members in the Gulf. Life was upset, and they were anxious. When something as prepossessing as a war happens, it's time for feeding.

I preached on how we should feel toward someone as hateful as Hussein, what to do for children watching war reports on television, how to pray for the troops to be victorious without being vindictive. In addition we conducted special prayer meetings on the war.

● *Listen for God's direction.* Although I'm attentive to the calendar cycles mentioned above, I don't want to become a slave to the church calendar. God sometimes leads me to do things that counter my assumptions.

Recently as I was praying over making a financial appeal, I saw in my mind a group of people in a rubber raft being carried through white water. I have never ridden a boat through rapids, so there was no reason for such an image to come to my mind; I felt the vision was from the Lord.

The boat was navigating a canyon with no room on either side to beach. I felt impressed that God was saying our church had a lot of things happening, so it was not the time to add more. We should just hold tight.

That was a difficult decision. Two years earlier we had spent $11 million on a church and campus; so people were still affected by that. But if we didn't challenge the congregation financially, we would lose a window of opportunity: Easter and a special denominational convention to be held at our church would soon crowd out any church business for several months.

But I decided to go with how I felt God leading me, and several weeks later, the Lord guided me to meet this need in another way. I gave myself to several weeks of prayer and then wrote a simple letter of explanation to the congregation.

In effect, I said, "We're all busy, and I haven't the heart to put something else on you. I'm simply asking you to pray and give as you feel directed."

I lead as I feel God directs, but not unless he confirms his direction through our leaders. I never unilaterally follow any impressions regarding the administrative path of the church.

I followed this procedure when our church purchased the church building and campus about half a mile from us.

That process began when I received a literal "word" from the Lord. When I presented the idea to our church, however, I didn't mention what God had revealed to me. If I had done that, the leaders might have been swayed by their trust in me and by my track record of God having led me in the past. Instead I presented the idea first to the elders of the church and to the pastoral staff, then to the 230 deacons, and finally to the congregation.

The elders appointed a task force to study the feasibility of the purchase, a committee from which I absented myself. I asked them to analyze the purchase without my input. Only after the final decision did I tell the congregation how the Lord had led me, and this only as an additional witness to them that God was in our decision. I felt that the Lord had indeed led me because *their* faith was aroused without any human manipulation.

The Sunday after the staff member acknowledged to me his moral failure, I announced to the congregation at the end of our morning services, "For the first time in my thirteen years as your pastor, we have had the heartbreaking experience of a moral difficulty with one of our pastoral team. We will address that tonight in our evening service."

That night the building was packed. I taught for fifty minutes on God's perfect design for sexual relationships and why our disobedience to that design hurts him and us. I explained what the Bible teaches about leaders who fall, about what their forgiveness does and doesn't mean.

Then we served Communion. With the bread in my hands, I talked about the brokenness of all our lives but especially how Jesus was broken on behalf of our brokenness. "What we are expecting tonight is wholeness," I said.

I took the cup in my hand and talked about the cleansing power of the blood of Christ.

Before we drank from the cup, I said, "The staff member who has admitted his moral failure has made clear his intention to turn from his action and seek restoration within the community life of this church." Then I called him by name to come forward.

I could hear people quietly weeping all over the auditorium.

He spoke for a few minutes and concluded with, "I ask you all to forgive me."

After I prayed over the cup, I put my arm around him. I asked everyone to stretch their hand toward him and in unison say, "John, I forgive you."

Their voices thundered the response, and we drank from the cup.

No one could have left that service feeling we had swept his failure under the rug or treated it as unoffensive to God. Nor could anyone leave without feeling a holy reverence for God.

Though always in tension, leading and feeding are not in opposition. When best expressed, we lead when we feed, and we feed when we lead. You can't fully do either alone.

In some ways pastors are called to a ministry style that invites confrontation and criticism. It's the nature of ministry.

— Ben Patterson

The Pastor as Lightning Rod

There she sat, nervously but methodically making her way through two pages of typewritten, single-spaced criticisms of our church office operation. To her credit, she met with me face to face, which is more than many critics are willing to do.

As she rehearsed the failures of the staff (and seemingly, everyone else born after the Spanish-American War) I felt increasingly melancholy. From improper procedures in answering the phone, to conflicting announcements in the bulletin, to secretaries breaching confidences, she had meticulously kept track of every offense. She had no less than fifty indictments.

When she was through, I did what pastors are supposed to do. I thanked her and affirmed her concern. After she left, I seriously considered conducting tours of the Holy Land for the rest of my career.

Why is it pastors so often serve as the lightning rod for the highly charged complaints and grievances of church members? Why do we attract criticisms that pulsate with gigawatts of negative energy? How do we protect ourselves from ecclesiastical electrocution? Can we transform these painful experiences from lethal discharges into spiritual energy and light?

High Pressure Systems

Upper air turbulence and the clash of competing weather fronts often produce violent and dangerous storms. In much the same way, unstable patterns and changing seasons in the church can produce high-voltage criticism. Some conditions in church life predictably produce more lightning.

● *Transitions.* When I began my ministry in a church that had been two years without a pastor, I noticed immediately how uncertain people seemed. If they were leaders in the old system, would they be trusted by the new? If they were good friends with Pastor Harry, would they enjoy the same relationship with me? In one way or another, all these insecurities became focused on me.

It wasn't long until twenty-five people joined another church, unhappy or uncertain of their place in the new order. I was blamed for their departure, though I didn't have a clue why they left. All they said was, "I don't think I fit in here anymore." What it felt like to me was, "Something is the matter since you've come."

I was a new pastor, I didn't know them; they didn't know me. And they knew I didn't know them. That's unsettling. It can produce sudden storms and foul weather before I even have the opportunity to unpack my furniture.

● *Financial difficulties.* When giving is down, trouble is usually up. Financial problems raise insecurities or frustrations that have been lying just beneath the surface of a church.

The most common result is the blame game, and the most logical "blamee" is the pastor. Blamers reason that people have quit giving because something is wrong, and it's up to leaders to keep things from going wrong, and therefore, what's wrong must be me. In its worst forms, angry parishioners will use a type of blackmail to get rid of the minister: they stop their giving, hoping to force the pastor out.

• *Projections and dependency.* For some people, I become a Rorschach inkblot: they see in me whatever it is that is troubling them.

A psychologist friend suggests that people's unresolved issues with their fathers make pastors a prime target for criticism. Either irrational anger or an inappropriate clinging is the tip-off. When someone clings, I instinctively retreat, and that makes the clinging individual angry.

At one church, one man began this pattern with me. He had been orphaned as a child. His mother had left him when he was young, and his father eventually passed him off to people who adopted him.

When I first met him, he had no beard. But within a couple of weeks of becoming friends, he began to grow one (I have a beard, too). Initially, he was my best friend. He was talented, intelligent, and loyal, and I was grateful for his acquaintance.

Over time I became uneasy about the demands he placed on me. We were having more lunches, breakfasts, and get-togethers than I could handle. Frankly, he became a nuisance. I attempted gently to put some distance between us, and he immediately picked up on it.

Something changed inside him. In less than a year, he went from ally to adversary. Soon he was opposing me on various issues, on any grounds he could dig up. The flip-flop was so obvious it was embarrassing. My two-cent Freudian analysis suggests that my backing off, however slight, made him feel orphaned once again.

• *Consumer mentality.* Churchgoers today often think of the pastor as performing a service for them. They are as demanding and particular as if they had bought a suit from a clothing store and didn't like the cuff length. If something doesn't meet their standards, they want to see the store manager and file a complaint. The result is a critical and demanding spirit. The woman with the two pages of complaints acted like a customer who was pointing out the faults in our service.

The Personal Pain of High-Voltage Criticism

When I was younger, I believed my ego strength could protect me from the pain of criticism. As I've gotten older, I've come to admit how much this stuff hurts. I wish I could become what some call a "non-anxious presence," but public and private criticism still unsettles me. When I'm criticized, I am subject to a variety of emotions.

Of all the jolts you take in the course of your ministry, perhaps none hurts more than having your character called into question. A pastor friend was confronted by a man who had a mile-long list of criticisms. My friend had tried previously to reconcile with the man over a few meals, but all he had to show for his efforts was heartburn.

My friend interrupted the attack: "Clearly, you think I'm doing everything wrong. But do you trust my heart?"

There was a long pause. The man looked at my friend and said, "No, I think you're trying to ruin the church." My friend was stunned.

Several months later, in a meeting with elders, this man appeared before the church elders with the same grocery list of complaints against the pastor. My friend asked him the same question, "Do you think I am trying to destroy the church?"

To the man's credit (at least he was honest), he said yes. Now the board sat astonished and speechless.

Even if I'm sure the person is wrong, when people question my character, it hurts. Our character and motives are two of the main things we offer a congregation. If character is questioned, the foundation of ministry is threatened. Frankly, I don't think anyone except a sociopath can take that type of heat from people and remain indifferent.

Then there is fear and rage. Though few people in my life have had the candor (or perhaps the audacity) to tell me I don't belong in the ministry, when it has happened, it has left me with a feeling of shame, mingled with anger.

If I'm tired and under stress, I can begin feeling like a failure. I doubt the very thing I've given my entire adult life to. I wonder if I'm losing it as pastor. The Enemy jumps on those situations to whisper, "Your critics are right, you know. You have no business being here. Cut your losses, and get out before you're humiliated big time."

If you're not careful, your mind can begin racing and creating frightening scenarios: *What if I have to move my family again? What if I can't get another job or provide for them? What if I end up on an ecclesiastical blacklist?* You begin imagining yourself ten years from now lying in an alley near a rescue mission, dead drunk, having lost your wife and family!

Then I can begin imploding. I blame myself for all that has happened. If only I had done this or that differently.

I don't know how common the emotion of rage is among pastors, but I struggle with it. When I've been told that my ministry is bogus, I want to shout my defense. Yet, because of my professional and family responsibilities, I'm not allowed to do that. And the anger inside me just keeps building.

Pastors also feel isolated. Once, after I took a particularly difficult emotional beating at the hands of a parishioner, I found no one I could talk to about it. That created a profound loneliness. While I could share my pain with my wife, it seemed a terribly heavy burden to ask her to carry. So I carried the incident inside for nearly four months.

That's often the catch-22 pastors find themselves in. They deal with issues far too difficult to walk through alone, yet if they share them with anyone else in the congregation, it can lead to church-wide division and possibly war.

I'm tempted to sit down during a staff meeting and rehearse the sordid details of someone's attack on me. But that only creates a fortress mentality among the staff, us against them.

Finally, we are subject to defensiveness. A woman in a congregation I served was criticizing my ministry. As we were trying to work out the problem, she said, "You have to be more receptive to what others want you to do" (translated, "You have to do exactly what I want you to do").

Instinctively, I decided *not* to do whatever she told me! Though in retrospect I see an element of truth to her comments, my own ego wouldn't allow me to admit it. I'd like to write off such people as incorrigible cranks.

What I need to do is forgive, to bless those who persecute me. But sometimes their actions eat away at my soul.

Preserving my own boundaries while forgiving those who violate them is an emotional and spiritual high-wire act.

Vital Circuit Breakers

Building codes require special electrical devices that prevent a surge of energy from overloading the circuits and leading to a meltdown and fire. These circuit breakers interrupt the dangerously high level of electricity in the line by providing relief from the excessive load.

In the same fashion, I've found I need emotional and spiritual circuit breakers to protect when highly charged criticism is directed at me.

● *Accepting who you are.* When a woman told me that I always wanted to do things my way, I had to agree with her. Knowing myself, my gifts and convictions, and God's call for my life has been absolutely essential to carrying me through the deep waters of ministry.

At age 50 I can say things with certainty about my life that I could not have said, nor should have, at age 25. There's a peace of mind that comes with twenty-five years of learning who you are. I possess reasonably good self-evaluation skills and a good deal of self-knowledge. I've come to know my deepest passions in ministry.

Furthermore, if I know God has called me to a particular place,

I can be assured that what I bring is what the church must need. Is that outrageous? Arrogant? If I *didn't* believe that, I would call the moving van every time I'm struck by lightning.

(The corollary, of course, is also true. If I find I can't do ministry the way God has called me to do it, then I must go elsewhere. And this for me is one test I use in determining when it's time to move on.)

● *The necessity of rest.* When fatigue creeps on you, it isn't long before your instincts start failing you. As Vince Lombardi said, "Fatigue makes cowards of us all." You start to lose focus. You begin to make unwise decisions. I say things in meetings when I'm tired that I would never say if I was refreshed and well-rested.

One annual meeting came at the end of a long week and full day. I remember thinking to myself, *I just want to get this stupid thing over with.* When people began throwing verbal tomatoes at the staff, I showed little patience. My answers were short and curt, with an edge of sarcasm. What the people saw that night was a tired, touchy, frustrated pastor. I think they would have seen someone entirely different if I had taken a nap that afternoon.

Can we be gentle and sensitive when we've worked 60, 70, or 80 hours that week? I no longer trivialize the importance of getting adequate rest. It's a cheap and simple fuse that can save me a great deal of trouble.

● *Keeping perspective on the 5 percent.* I'm amazed at what 5 percent of the congregation can do to my perception of ministry. In the calm light of day, I can see that the overwhelming majority of the church is happy, contented, and sailing down the highway on cruise control. Yet, if I'm not careful, I can let the one nasty look or the one vindictive letter change how I see everything.

Several years ago psychologist Albert Ellis said that it is irrational to believe that every significant person in your community must like you before you can feel good about yourself. He is right, particularly in a church setting.

● *The power of a prayer journal.* The biggest mistake I've made through the years is to turn my feelings in on myself, allowing them to implode. I now turn them into dialogue with God, and I do that with a prayer journal.

I use the journal to record the feelings and thoughts that are stirring in my soul. I lay them out before God where I don't have to hide anything. When I feel betrayed, or my anguish is overwhelming, I'll mirror that before God.

I often allow the Psalms to become my discussion with God, "Contend, O Lord, with those who contend against me." My feelings are transformed into dialogue with God. That's so much better than talking to myself, or even laying it all on my wife.

Later, when I've resolved a particular crisis, I like to go back and read the chronicles of my struggle. Seeing how I navigated heavy weather two years earlier, helps me weather my current storm.

● *Memorizing comfort.* When I was young, I never won any awards for Sunday school Scripture memory contests. Someone else always rode away on the ten-speed bicycle at the end of the year. But in the last three years I've discovered that Scripture can give voice to things I don't know how to express. It transforms the things churning inside me and brings real healing to my soul.

One summer I memorized the twelfth chapter of Hebrews. At the time the entire chapter seemed autobiographical: running the race set before us, remembering Jesus, who endured the cross, who didn't lose heart though scorned by men. The chapter reminded me that pain is a discipline God uses in my life: I was in training, and the pain caused by criticism was my coach.

● *Finding Aaron and Hur.* Every pastor needs an Aaron and Hur, like the two men of Israel who held up the arms of Moses in the battle against the Amalekites (Ex. 17:8–13).

When I arrived at one church, I met two men who introduced themselves by saying, "We're here to pray for you." From that point on, they were up at six o'clock every Saturday morning to pray on my behalf.

The Aarons and Hurs in my life have seldom, if ever, been aware of the machinations going on within the church, but their prayers have helped me weather many storms.

● *The support of family.* When one presidential candidate announced his withdrawal from the race, he was asked if he was deeply disappointed.

"No," he replied, "but my 10-year-old daughter is. She said she believes if people knew how wonderful her dad was they'd certainly vote for him."

That's the type of support every pastor needs. And I have no better supporter than my wife, Loretta. I'm reminded of a cartoon in which a minister is sitting in his living room on a Sunday afternoon sucking his thumb. His wife, obviously attempting to comfort him says, "Yes, honey. Your sermon was just fine." I turn to my wife for comfort when I'm feeling overwhelmed by the insecurities and anxieties the pastorate produces.

Once during a particularly difficult time in our ministry, we took a trip that covered a large portion of the northern United States and Canada. We were driving through a marvelous portion of a wooded landscape. It was late in the afternoon, and the sun was low, setting the horizon on fire with shades of purple, red, and orange.

We were listening to a tape by Garrison Keillor. He described a scene in which a husband and wife are sitting across the breakfast table from one another. The husband is a mess; he has the flu. The pressures in his life are making him sick. The story ends by Keillor telling how his wife reached across the table, took his hand, and said, "You know, I care for you." In his deep baritone fashion he concluded by saying, "And you know, sometimes that's enough."

Loretta and I were feeling the burden and the sorrow of having served as lightning rods for so many months at our church. We reached out and held each other's hands as the story ended. It was a wonderful moment.

Harnessing the Energy of the Critics

The same water that, unchecked, uproots trees and floods a town can, when channeled, light a city. As frustrating and difficult as it is to serve as the lightning rod for a congregation, it does have its useful side.

We ought to worry, in fact, if we never receive a zap now and then. If I can't remember the last time I was criticized for something, chances are I'm not doing anything significant. If my goal is simply to keep all the cattle mooing softly in the corral, I'm failing as a leader. But if you are moving them out on the trail toward Dodge City and points beyond, you can expect an occasional stampede or two. It comes with the territory of leadership.

I think of Moses. Half the time he was talking the Lord out of killing the people. The other half, God was trying to talk Moses out of doing them in.

I remind myself that negative energy is to be preferred to no energy at all. The only organisms with no energy are dead.

I do, though, try to limit *public* attacks. In public, all eyes are upon you, and the temptations to get defensive and overreact are enormous. I'd much rather hear a complaint one on one. Then I can ask questions and clarify matters with more freedom. Sometimes you have to teach a church how to do this.

A friend of mine served a church with a tradition he found unsettling: the annual congregational meeting was consumed with an inordinate amount of griping and complaining. My friend thought the meeting ought to be an occasion to celebrate God's goodness. But his congregation assumed this was the time to get everything off its chest, even if it meant publicly attacking an individual. My friend kept calling people out of order for criticizing the staff; the congregation kept getting frustrated because they thought that's what the meeting was for.

Eventually, the leadership of the church challenged the people first to go directly to the persons with whom they had disputes. They outlined a step-by-step approach to resolving conflict that only as a last resort involved bringing the matter to the public attention of the congregation.

Furthermore, the people were told that if they brought up a public complaint at the annual meeting, they would be asked if they first had followed the procedure. The public attacks at the annual meeting were cut significantly.

I also try to listen to Balaam's donkey. It was the nineteenth-century pastor and writer George MacDonald who said, "Truth is truth, whether it's spoken by the lips of Jesus or Balaam's donkey." In the midst of even the most withering criticism, I need to stop and listen for the grain of truth. Granted, it may come across as unfair, judgmental, and cruel, but underneath the rough exterior there may be something of value.

This is especially true if an issue keeps surfacing. If people say repeatedly, "We feel you don't care about us pastorally," it likely indicates people are feeling lonely and in need of spiritual support. That doesn't mean *I* have to become more pastoral — make more hospital calls, arrange more counseling sessions. But I better make sure that somebody is doing that sort of thing.

Sometimes, of course, there's nothing better I can do than simply apologize. At my last church, I suggested that we add a third service to our Sunday morning schedule. Although there wasn't much enthusiasm for the idea, my attendance projections indicated we could support a third service. I enthusiastically pushed the new schedule through staff, elder, and congregational meetings.

After a few months on the new schedule, attendance continued to sag. Finally, a good friend told me the truth, "Ben, the numbers just don't support that type of change. You really should have done your homework first." I was angry at him, but I was forced to be more thorough about my original calculations. Sure enough, he was right. I remember distinctly how I felt at the time: stupid.

I began to see all the administrative pain I had caused choirs and church school teachers. I felt like quitting and entering a remote desert monastery. But that was not the time to flee. Instead, I simply admitted to the board that I had blown it and began taking administrative steps to return to two services.

After one horrible defeat, in which he lost thousands of men, General Ulysses Grant was seen going into his tent that night to cry uncontrollably for nearly an hour — he'd made some strategic blunders that needlessly cost men their lives.

But the next day, his men saw him emerge with the determined look of a general. He calmly mounted his horse and continued on with his campaign.

That is the type of resolute courage I want to have even when I've deservedly been struck by lightning.

Pain Is the Diploma

My seminary degree and my years in the pastorate don't authenticate my ministry, not at least according to the apostle Paul. He believed his apostleship was validated by the sufferings and hardships he had endured: shipwrecks, beatings, hunger, and rejection. In some ways pastors are called to a ministry style that invites confrontation and criticism. It's the nature of our calling.

I don't want to rationalize insensitivity or poor leadership as prophetic ministry. Yet, as I look back, I've often been placed in situations where new foundations needed to be laid. That often involves shaking things up.

I can't serve God and play it safe. The risk of criticism and misunderstanding is the price of a pastor's life, a life filled with dreams and visions of what God wants to do next. It's a risk I'm willing to take.

Part 2
Working with the Congregation

Get the right people in the right positions to begin with. Motivating people who fit their jobs is much easier than hassling with those who buck the system.

— *Leith Anderson*

CHAPTER FOUR

When You Need to Motivate — or Correct

I once invited a well-known preacher and educator to speak at a Christian education banquet held at our church. An hour and a half before the event, I learned our Sunday school superintendent, a main figure on the evening's program, would not be attending. He was protesting the presence of our "theologically liberal" guest speaker.

I picked up the phone.

"Bob, I understand you don't feel comfortable with our speaker's theological convictions," I said.

"Uh, yes."

"In the spirit of Matthew 18, then, can I ask you several questions? Have you confronted him personally with your concerns? If so, have you met with him again, taking along a member of the church? Finally, if you were unsatisfied with the results of your first two meetings, did you request that the matter be brought before the church?"

A long silence screamed from the other end of the line. "No," he admitted reluctantly.

"If you follow through with your protest," I said, "I believe you'll be going contrary to clear biblical teaching. Unless you follow these biblical guidelines in the next hour, then, I hope you'll fulfill your duties at the banquet."

To his credit, the superintendent showed up with his game face and managed to endure the program. Not much later, however, he resigned.

His behavior was inappropriate. But it would have been more inappropriate to let it slide. He needed to be held accountable.

Situations like this are always gut wrenching. But they're part of church ministry. Do it well, and the church hums; do it poorly, and programs crawl, people fume, efficiency grinds to a halt.

I'd much rather the staff, lay leaders, and congregation did the right thing every time. To avoid having to correct, I try to put in place a system that will motivate people to do the right thing.

Simple Maintenance

As a young pastor, a problem individual in the church continually plagued me and my ministry. No one, including me, knew what to do with him. Exasperated, I finally encouraged him to serve on the board. I reasoned that if he was on the board, at least I could keep an eye on him.

What a perfectly awful experiment. He sabotaged good ideas, obstructed vision, and initiated fruitless debate; he wound up being a bigger problem on the board.

Such pain can be redeemed. In this case, I learned a life-long lesson: get the right people in the right positions to begin with. Motivating people who fit their jobs is much easier than hassling with those who chafe and buck the system. To bypass a world of frustration, invest heavily in people *before* they become leaders.

That's one reason I *always* attend nominating committee meetings, taking a pro-active role in the discussions. The committees probably get bored with my opening speech, in which I discuss church philosophy, the right way to select good candidates, and leadership expectations. But laying that groundwork helps us choose the right people.

I read excerpts from 1 Timothy 3 regarding the biblical criteria for leadership. Then I move on to our church constitution, not exactly scintillating prose, but a clear statement of our church's mission. I cap my presentation with stories that show the value of choosing the right people.

I also guide the committee as it makes specific selections, although that can be awkward. Once I was late for a nominating committee meeting. The meeting already in session, I stepped in the room, noticing a number of names of possible candidates written on the board.

Halfway through the list, my heart sank. One of the names was a man accused of sexually molesting his child. Criminal charges were being considered against him.

No one on the committee was aware of the serious allegations. Stomach churning, I agonized for forty-five minutes, trying to decide the best course of action. I couldn't reveal this privileged information, but neither could I allow his name to stand. I gulped and made my stand.

"Before I came in, you wrote a number of names on the board," I said with an artificial calm. "I don't feel comfortable with one of them. I'd like it removed."

"Which one is it?" the chairman replied innocently. I said the name.

The chairman simply went to the board and erased the name. No one blinked; no one asked why. I had just experienced the equivalent of an ecclesiastical near miss in midair. As I touched down, I quietly resolved not to be late for another nominating committee, nor ever allow names to be randomly listed for office.

An ounce of prevention is worth a pound of emotional agony. That's why I invest a significant amount of time preparing for those meetings. By design, the chairman of the board and I are automatic members of the nominating committee. That authorizes us to meet in advance, discussing individuals whom we might nominate.

Before a name reaches the blackboard, we consider each person thoroughly. We request reviews of their giving record, their membership history, and their qualifications for office. By weighing information about individuals, we exert a strong influence on the names that finally appear on the ballot.

Yet even before the nominating committee, we're developing leaders. Like a baseball farm system, future leaders must do well in AA ball if they hope to move up to AAA competition. By watching them in the minors, we can eventually tell whether they have the desire and skills to play major league ball.

The best indicator of future performance is past performance. Potential tells little about an individual; past behavior speaks volumes. Observing people over an extended period of time is the best predictor of future fitness for leadership.

Our standard practice is to give potential leaders opportunities to serve in a number of roles. They might first serve on a task force. Next, they might teach a class. Then they might be named to head up a special project.

During this time, I'm asking several questions: Can this person think conceptually? Does this person share the vision of the church? Is he spiritually mature and growing? Is she trustworthy?

When we're ready to ask a person to take significant responsibility, we have two further criteria. First, we believe ministry takes precedence over position. We're not looking to fill slots; rather we search for people already active in ministry. One man turned down an opportunity to serve on the elder board because he believed it would interrupt his boys ministry on Wednesday nights. Ironically, that's the type of person we're looking for — someone who values ministry over position.

We also see if people demonstrate leadership before they are appointed to it. The reverse — position first, then ability — is often disappointing, if not catastrophic. Positions normally don't shape a person, the person makes the position.

The pressures and demands of top-level leadership are great. Leaders need the incubation process to mature. Our desire is to be a pennant team, and our farm club system gives us an opportunity to discover those who will be future champions.

Finally, I realize that good boards come in small packages. I once asked a pastor how many members were on his board.

"Twenty-five," he replied.

"You don't have twenty-five leaders in your church."

"You're right. How did you know?" he asked.

"Because there aren't twenty-five leaders in the country. Even if there were, they couldn't all be in your church."

I was joking, of course, but I was aiming at a crucial principle: there are limited numbers of top-caliber leaders in any one church. Boards that become too large stretch their leadership resources. Creating too many slots with too few qualified people to fill them is a formula for frustration. I prefer quality over quantity. If the church constitution calls for twenty-five members on the board, I'd suggest lobbying to change the constitution instead of beating the bushes for prospective leaders who don't exist.

See You at the Top

When a British mountain climber scaling Mount Everest perished, a member of the expedition recorded in his diary a fitting epilogue: "He was last seen heading for the top."

I hope the same could one day (later rather than sooner) be said of my life. In fact, I hope that it could be said of our entire church staff and leadership. High ministry standards are an integral part of our church identity. We deliberately instill the values of pursuing excellence, reward for strong efforts, and applaud visionary decision making. Here are a few practices I follow to keep people heading for the top.

● *Practice affirming actions.* One Easter Sunday our music director arranged for the orchestra to accompany the opening hymn. It was a magnificent addition to worship. However, the plan called for the orchestra to be dismissed before the sermon. After the first service, I realized the mistake. The last hymn sounded flat as a North Dakota interstate. We needed the instruments for the final hymn.

But time was running out. That morning we had four services, each ten minutes apart. Making a last-minute decision, I dashed out into the hallway, searching for our music director. I knew I was asking the impossible.

"Dave," I said, "I need to ask you a big favor. The last hymn went flat without the orchestra. Can you gather the orchestra together in time to perform in the next service?"

Without batting an eye, he replied, "I'll have them assembled for the next service." When the orchestra finished accompanying the last hymn, not one soul in the congregation knew what a musical feat had just been accomplished.

In next morning's staff meeting, I couldn't wait to tell the others of Dave's effort the day before.

"I asked Dave to do the impossible yesterday, and he did it. Few music ministers in this country could say to their musicians, 'We need you to play a hymn next hour without rehearsing it.' "

I like to catch people doing things right, and then publicly affirm them. It keeps high-motivation octane in their fuel tank. I'm always amazed how far a person will travel on a gallon of praise.

● *Invest in the bond market.* Another key element in motivating people is the development of close, supportive, and caring relationships. I let our staff and lay leadership know that I'm available when they need me. But I also let them know I need them.

I have opened my private life to the elders. I share my family struggles and sorrows. I don't hide the fact I'm not a perfect parent or spouse. I have sought their counsel in personal financial decisions. Before buying our summer cottage, I asked, "What does buying a cabin communicate to the congregation? Does it send a wrong message?"

I had no desire to appear extravagant or elitist. Even though owning a summer cabin is common for many middle-income families in Minnesota, I wanted to check in. I've asked for advice before buying a car. Because they know my heart, I can trust their mind in these matters.

We use other methods to develop close bonds. Every other month, I invite the staff and elder board to our home for a game night. They take over the house. Some use the trampoline, others watch the big-screen television, while still others shoot hoops. In the summer, I invite leaders to our cottage. In each case the strategy and objective is the same: to build a team by simply having fun together.

On a spiritual level, we cement relationships by making a mutual commitment to pray daily for each other. Though I rarely make hospital calls, I'll visit an elder who is ill or facing surgery. I'll drop everything. During one elder's hospitalization, I called him three times the same day during an especially busy day. He knew where my heart was.

● *Be up front about the stakes.* Leading a church forward is like playing in the majors. There are enormous rewards: the pay is good, the championship rings are impressive, and your picture appears on baseball cards. But there are tremendous pressures. You are expected to play as a professional on a daily basis.

When I share that analogy with my staff and elders, I'm not issuing a veiled threat: hit a home run or find another team. Rather, I'm trying to show them the stakes in rising to high levels of leadership. The rewards are great, but the price is a commitment to excellence and professionalism.

● *Help people be all they can be.* I believe competition in a church can be healthy. I'm not talking about trying to preach a better sermon than an associate. I'm referring to encouraging workers to compete with themselves. I want individuals to push the limits of their talents. I want our music to sound better this year than it did last year. I want our Christian education program to introduce new courses, drawing on the latest advances in the field. Throughout our programs, I push people to become all that God intended. Each component contributes to our larger goal of performing well as a team.

One of our staff members just completed her doctorate. Though she was never required to do so, we had encouraged her to pursue further education. We gave her time and paid for her research project — with no strings attached. Now that she's finished, she could take her degree and pursue greener pastures elsewhere. I don't want her to leave. But we don't strike deals to hold people. Instead we try to seek what's best for everyone. If we get to enjoy the benefits of our investment, so much the better.

And whenever possible, I like to find new positions within the church for those restless for change. Our evangelism pastor was once the junior high minister. He did an excellent job but outgrew the position. Sensing he was ready for a new challenge, I said, "Give me one more year, and I'll find another job for you."

He asked to preach more, so we gave him more pulpit time. He wanted further education, so we gave him time off to pursue a doctorate on the West Coast. He wanted broader horizons, so we sent him to Romania on a short-term assignment. I know he has large churches approach him to be their senior pastor. But he stays on.

The same principle applies in working with lay leadership. Watching some of our leaders begin a daughter church was exhilarating. We sent over people who were products of our "farm club" system to form the nucleus of the new church's elder board. We gave up precious leadership, but in the end it benefited everyone. They got off to a healthy start; we had the joy of starting a new witness for Christ.

● *Remember everyone's a volunteer.* Peter Drucker points out that all organizations, at their core, are volunteer organizations. We have to forget the idea there's a difference between paid staff and volunteers. If people don't enjoy doing what you ask, salaried or not, they'll quit and go elsewhere.

Although we try to pay our staff well, I know salaries alone won't motivate them to excellence. Money is never a sufficient reward to keep someone on the job. People need other incentives, such as self-esteem, a sense of accomplishment, and the satisfaction of sacrificing for a worthy cause.

Organized Accountability

Even if all leaders are highly qualified people, the time will come when we need correction. Fallible people make fallible judgments. What matters most, then, is dealing with errors constructively.

First, standards of excellence need to be established. Expectations need to be clearly communicated. Scripture needs to be recognized as the source of our operating principles. Actions perceived as arbitrary and personal can lead to division, acrimony, and poor performance. A "systems approach" to correction provides the safeguards of fairness, consistency, and objectivity.

Not all expectations are communicated in print. After working at Wooddale for a month or so, a new staff member gets the idea that punctuality is one of our standards: people make a strong effort to be on time to meetings, rarely being late. In some instances, the corporate culture corrects people who start to become tardy. The tardy person just senses that others, although understanding, really don't like waiting to start a meeting.

Other times a direct confrontation is necessary. But it doesn't have to be formal or made into a big deal.

One Easter Sunday we had a musical faux pas. The choir processional was a hymn that neither I nor the congregation could sing. Our standard of excellence in worship suffered.

At the time, I thought it the most unsingable melody in Protestantism. Adding salt to the wound, there was no printed music for people to follow, only words in the bulletin. We stumbled so badly that some people were chuckling. That wasn't the way I had hoped to begin the worship services of the biggest Sunday of the church year.

Talking to the music leader, I said, "Please, don't misunderstand me. I know you put time and preparation into planning the music. But why in the world did you choose that particular melody for the opening hymn?"

"I know it quite well," he said.

"Well, you may be the only person in the congregation who knows exactly how to sing it," I replied. We both smiled. The next time we sang a hymn from the hymnbook.

I was upset with the poor start, but I wasn't angry at him personally. I told him my concerns, and that was the end of the matter.

I want to correct behavior, not people. Correcting people is never easy, nor is it usually pleasant. When I have to confront a person who has done something wrong, I sometimes lie awake thinking about it. I'll stew about it. But I won't let it slide. Eventually, I'll confront the problem.

And when I do, my desire is to confront the person in a Christian manner, trusting the truth spoken in love will perform a good work in their lives. I try to show intolerance toward wrong behavior and tolerance for the individual, regardless of what's been done. Through the years I've seen patience change people's lives.

I once faced a woman who wanted me out of the church. She said so publicly. She accused me of greed and egotism because of a building program I had helped initiate. She wasn't really a threat, but she annoyed me and others. Sadly, she was a troubled person wrestling with numerous unresolved issues in her life.

Rather than isolate or ignore her, I spent a great deal of time talking with her about her concerns while I let her know I thought her attacks out of place. I sent her notes and letters, even after I was called to another church. Eventually, she changed, and today we are friends.

Sometimes, of course, correction is not enough. Peter Drucker believes that every time an organization doubles in size, half its leaders become obsolete for their positions. I've asked Wooddale's leadership, "We had X number of people in our worship service last Sunday. If you want to double that number, at least half of us will not be competent to lead a church of that size. Are you willing to pay that price?"

Most agree in principle, but the rub comes when personnel

change becomes necessary. Letting people go is perhaps the most unpleasant task of leadership. The final decision is often agonizing to everyone involved. If the individual has been loyal, hard working, and well-liked by the people, the decision is more painful.

Here's where leaders must make tough calls. Even though people may be well-intentioned and diligent, if they don't possess the needed skills to move the church forward, a change is needed. Loyalty is a virtue, but blind loyalty can hinder ministry.

Still, I'm repulsed by the idea that people should be used until they outlive their usefulness and then simply discarded. Christian grace calls for showing as much concern for the person's next position as we did in bringing him or her on staff in the first place.

Let My People Go

Through motivation and correction, I hope to further the work of the church and set people free. If correction binds people from fulfilling their objectives, something is seriously wrong.

Conducting church business in the proper way ought to liberate people. I'm optimistic that our approach is achieving that end. A man with a business degree from a major Midwestern university said to me, "I learned more about solid business practices by attending the church than I did from my four years in college."

My desire is to see people motivated, and if need be, corrected in order for our church to serve God with all of our heart, mind, and soul. Whether we or another church are the direct beneficiary of our efforts doesn't matter. If God's kingdom advances, and Christ is glorified, we have made it to the top.

Mistrust of leadership has reached pandemic proportions.
— Ben Patterson

Leading
Reluctant Followers

Some people become reluctant followers early in life. I know I did.

I was just 8 years old when my uncle convinced me that if I sat on top of the roof, held my breath, and jumped off, I would float down. I believed him. Fortunately nothing was broken — except my ability to trust people.

I'm not the only reluctant follower. Since becoming a pastor, I've realized how difficult it is for some people to trust the church's leadership. At times, such mistrust can get out of hand.

One evening a member of our board was presenting a proposal to the annual meeting. In the middle of her presentation, several people actually began booing her. The hissing and catcalls were a scene right out of the English Parliament. I was stunned by their behavior. I wanted to drag the hecklers outside. The entire incident reminded me again that those most in need of leadership are often the ones most opposed to it.

Sometimes reluctance to follow serves a congregation well — not everything a pastor says should be taken as straight from the mouth of God. Yet, overall I am disturbed by the trend I see in our culture. Mistrust of leadership has reached pandemic proportions. I regularly meet people who've learned mistrust as a lifestyle. They've been hurt by the people they should have been able to believe. They can't defer to anyone now. They've become trust-impaired.

In the church the result is strangulation. Members can't follow the lead of a pastor or board. The pastor, for instance, is given enormous responsibility but little authority. We're called on to save the world, but we can't distribute ten dollars from the benevolence fund without calling a board meeting.

The proliferation of church committees is a sign of this trend. Committees tend to diffuse authority throughout the church. That may empower the laity, but the church can nearly grind to a halt over relatively insignificant decisions. You can't paint the library without checking with the Christian education committee (which oversees the library), the youth group (which meets in the library for Sunday school), the building and grounds committee (which monitors the building), and the budget committee (which authorizes money for painting). Naturally, if the young couples group is going to do the painting, you'll have to check with them as well!

But such is the culture we try to minister in today. We're called by God to lead a people who don't seem to want to be led. It's not a new problem; Moses faced it long ago. And it is a problem that can be effectively dealt with. Here's how I've tried.

Encouraging Followership

Since we can no longer assume that people want to follow our leadership, we need to encourage them to do so. At a minimum, that means not putting stumbling blocks in their way. But it also means setting a tone to my ministry that will entice people to follow.

● *Don't butcher the sacred cows.* People will not follow us if they sense we're trying to rustle their sacred cows. Knowing that, early on I try to discover the location of that herd. That's difficult sometimes because most sacred cows are invisible ground round — they aren't easily identified. The moment I stumble into a corral of sacred cows, though, I know it.

For example, I served a church with a long history of faith pledging, in which people promise in their hearts, though not on paper, what they'll give for the coming year. Wanting to plan wisely for the coming year, I thought it would be good to get some indication of what we could expect from the congregation. So at one board meeting, I asked the elders each to write down what they gave to the church the previous year. I might as well have asked them to undress publicly. In the quiet, frozen atmosphere of the room, I distinctly heard the mooing of sacrosanct bovines.

"Okay," I said with a smile, "I see I must be careful when we start talking about stewardship." Polite laughter around the room put the matter to pasture.

● *Get your board on board.* Perhaps the most crucial element in successfully winning the congregation's support is to get the board behind you. Leaders have a great deal of latitude as long as they enjoy the board's support. If the congregation understands the board is foursquare behind the pastor, they will fall in line.

As a young pastor I was naive about this. I thought it was enough to get "the people" behind me. But "the people" is an ill-defined group. It's far more important that I have the solid support of the elders, who will provide a buffer when the criticism comes. As Proverbs says, four things move with stately bearing: a lion, a strutting rooster, a he-goat, and a pastor surrounded by his elder board!

As a result I spend a majority of my time with three groups in the church: my staff, the elders (board members), and developing leaders. The latter group will one day be my board, and it's vital that

I begin building relationships long before they reach the board.

● *Listen for the personal dimension.* A few years ago, an elder on our board resigned, claiming he was under-utilized by the church. That made me angry. He had a history of dropping the ball whenever he was given an assignment. It was ridiculous for this irresponsible person to accuse others of failing to recognize his gifts.

When we finally got together to talk things out, I thought I needed to exert strong leadership, to hold this man accountable. But I lost it. I just chewed the man out. It took a year before we could speak about this incident again.

That's when I found out that during the time leading up to his departure from the church, his marriage was falling apart. He was angry that we hadn't noticed, but then, he hadn't told us. Still I felt badly that I hadn't thought to go beyond his public reasons for quitting.

Not every situation in the church calls for strong, dynamic leadership. Often the pastoral touch is the most effective way of building trust in your leadership.

● *Lead boldly and let grace abound.* Even though I know people are hesitant to follow, I'm not hesitant to lead. In fact, if I were hesitant, it would undermine my credibility. So I have to make tough decisions and voice my opinion about the direction of the church, albeit with some discretion at first.

Still, at times pastors must act on their best instincts and leave the results with God, particularly when the issues are not clear-cut. It's what Martin Luther referred to as "sinning boldly" in the gray areas of life.

I'm not always 100 percent certain I'm doing the right thing, so I'll often find myself praying, "Lord have mercy on me" or "If I'm wrong about this, please redeem it."

A decisive leader who occasionally makes mistakes is to be preferred to a paralyzed individual who fears a misstep. The difference between General George McClellan and General Ulysses Grant was simple: each commanded a vast army, but one was afraid to use that command; the other was not.

Especially Good Times for Leading

Part of the discretion I use has to do with timing. Not every issue needs bold leadership from the pastor. But sometimes it's best to flex my leadership muscles a little more, times when even reluctant followers appreciate leadership.

● *The paradox of the new kid on the block.* A congregation is most eager to follow my lead when they are also the least apt to follow it — when I'm new. When I plot two lines on a graph, one for the willingness of a congregation to follow a pastor's leadership and one for its level of trust in him or her, I find several fascinating trends.

First, in our early years we find great expectation and excitement, which translates into eagerness regarding our fresh ideas. But our chief asset, our newness, is also our chief liability. No one knows us, so few people trust us. So while eagerness is sky-high, the trust level lies on the bottom of the graph.

As the years go by, however, our trust level rises while our leadership punch sags. The reason for less leadership octane is institutional contentment. I find that once churches adjust to who I am and what I believe in, they become content with the way things are. They know me well, and they're happy with the status quo. So there just doesn't seem to be much reason to change anything.

If familiarity breeds a certain contempt when it comes to the willingness to follow, one antidote is to maintain a certain mystique. Great football coaches, for example, keep themselves aloof from their players, their staff, and the fans. You almost get the feeling these coaches watch the game from the highest seat in the stadium.

I don't want to become aloof. In fact, some of my colleagues think I err on the other side — they say I'm too open with my congregation. It's a thin tightrope to walk, but I never want to reveal so much of myself that my congregation can predict what I'm going to say or do next.

● *Healthy desperation.* Churches are usually ready to set aside their reluctance to follow when they experience healthy desperation. The church has fallen on hard times. Giving has collapsed.

Membership had dropped and the avalanche hasn't slowed. If a plane bounces through heavy turbulence, people will reach for their seat belts when the captain flashes the buckle-up light.

I recently received an inquiry letter from a church with a great history. One pastor served the church for several decades. Within three years of his retirement, though, the place began unraveling. The people cherish the memory of the former church, and now they're in pain. They're ready to trust a pastor who can show them the way out.

A word of warning: churches that have experienced nothing but grief and desperation for years are just about impossible to turn around. Certainly, a supernatural working of the Spirit can accomplish it, but not much else. Usually, such churches can be only maintained and take decades to move forward once again.

● *Good enemies produce strong allies.* A neighborhood petition, a zoning board fight, or a caustic article in the newspaper can galvanize a congregation behind the pastor. A good enemy will unify people behind a leader. While certain radio and television preachers seem to create (and exploit) a "crisis of the month" to boost donations, a realistic threat from the outside will almost always draw the congregation to the pastor.

● *A grand project.* If the program or plan is big enough, people feel over their heads, and they are more willing to be led.

Building projects are sometimes used in this way, though I'm cautious at this point. They are long and exhausting ordeals. They can come around and bite a pastor before he or she knows it. I recently read of a large church that received incredibly bad press because a mud slide from its building project blocked a road. A driver lost control, and there was a minor accident. The paper depicted the church as environmentally insensitive. Building projects can find a hundred ways to break your heart.

One of my experiences in California was just the opposite. Everyone knew we needed a building, everyone wanted one, and the church supported my leadership. It turned out to be a marvelously unifying experience. And we had few complications unlike the church above! But I tend to believe our experience was rare.

● *The right age and size.* I've also found that age can be an asset in persuading people to follow my lead. I jokingly advise others that it helps not to be too young or too old.

My own strength as a leader seemed to take a quantum leap when I hit age 40 to 45. I was no longer seen as the young kid with great potential and rough edges. At the same time they weren't expecting me to have a cardiac arrest any day. In some ways, I have reached the summer of my life. Maturity doesn't necessarily come with age, but it doesn't come without it either.

The size of a congregation can also affect your ability to lead. Lyle Schaller's book, *Looking in the Mirror*, details the changing dynamics of church leadership according to the size of the congregation. For instance, small churches, which he describes as "cats," can be particularly difficult to lead. Like felines, they do what they please, with no regard for anyone else's wishes, let alone the pastor's. They are so small, everyone feels as if they own the church — and practically speaking, it appears they do. They can operate with or without a pastor, and they know it.

My experience in California, of growing a church from approximately 60 people to 700, allowed me to glimpse firsthand the various leadership passages a church goes through. The easiest stage to exert leadership was from approximately 150 to 550 people. At that size it was just large enough to recognize its need for someone to give clear direction.

As it passed the 600 mark, though, I noticed little duchies began forming. City-states began declaring their independence and carefully guarding their turf. One city-state was composed of charismatics, another of those deeply committed to foreign missions, and so on.

Strangely enough, the small and large church share something in common: they're both hard to lead. If smaller churches are independent, larger ones are fragile and require skillful leadership to avoid fracturing. Whereas financial or attendance tremors may temporarily rattle a small church, they can produce high-end-Richter-scale damage in a huge congregation.

What They Say Is Not What They Mean

To become a good leader, you have to distinguish between what people say they want and what they really want. In counseling it's called the difference between the "presenting issue" and the "real issue."

For example, one couple in my church had a passion for the pro-life movement. Since I shared their convictions on the issue, I was eager to help them. What I didn't understand at the time was the wife's true motive.

Her husband was reluctant to get involved in our church. Because he didn't respond to Sunday school, small groups, or evening pot-luck dinners, she decided to use his commitment to pro-life to bring him into the church, through the back door, so to speak.

I thought they were involved because of their respect for life. Instead, it had to do with their marriage. When I tried to provide direction for their cause, I ran into problems. I was increasingly spending time in their home for one meeting after another. Finally, I had to back away, explaining that I couldn't give so much time to one cause. Eventually, I sorted things out and realized the woman had been using me, the church, and pro-life.

The whole episode reminded me of what the Gospel of John said about Jesus: he didn't entrust himself to others because he knew what was in their hearts. While I'm not entirely certain how to apply that truth to my life, I now move much slower when people ask for my leadership. I listen to see whether people want me to lead them or simply get behind them. If they've outlined everything they wish to do and how they're going to do it, I'm cautious: they may want support rather than direction. On the other hand, if they have a burden to do ministry but desperately need help organizing their efforts and ambitions, they need a leader.

Transformational Leadership

With all that said, I believe there are immense possibilities for providing leadership that people will respond to, and with integrity and enthusiasm.

Leighton Ford, in his book *Transforming Leadership*, stresses the difference between managers and transformational leaders. Managers attempt to do things right, while leaders are those who try to do the right thing. Leadership includes the ability to present a compelling vision to people. When people have a vision, you can withstand all manner of problems, glitches, and screw-ups. It's like an orchestra that recovers from a sour note or two — together they go on and finish the symphony.

Here are some things I keep in mind as I try to practice transformational leadership.

● *The vision thing.* It is thrilling to be able to share with a congregation an outline for future ministry, especially if it promises to transform people's lives: "Here's where we can go as a church, and here's why I think we should go there."

When I began a new church development in California, we began services for a small nucleus of people, and three months into the venture, I suggested having a membership class. The people responded with an enthusiasm that left me dizzy. Out of ninety or so people attending the church, eighty enrolled in the class.

There I laid out my vision for the church and its future. In those days, I took a prophetic stand against the materialism and hedonism of the Southern California culture that surrounded us. I urged that we become a body of believers that would carefully think through our life together. I appealed to the group to spend their money in ways that glorified God rather than fed an insatiable appetite for more and more toys.

I was thrilled to preach freely like that. That preaching energy coupled with a willing congregation proved synergistic. The commitment to a simple life and the level of giving was extraordinary. The congregation seemed to enjoy following as much as I enjoyed leading.

As a church we were self-consciously countercultural. The timing was right; the antiestablishment sentiment ruled the land from San Francisco to Woodstock. We offered people a chance to fulfill their unspoken dreams. Many of our people had become disillusioned with large, wealthy churches, which they had just left.

That vision didn't last, as none do. But that vision at that time helped me to lead and people to follow.

In my current setting, vision is summarized by the slogan, "To the Village and Beyond." The church is nearly two-and-a-half centuries old, so the challenge is to transform a village with a private, rural history into a dynamic body that can impact the great metroplexes that touch our community (New York City, in particular). I am urging the people to allow our church to become a center of renewal and mission to the massive urban areas right at our doorstep.

● *Assure the flock the pastures will stay green.* People might intellectually agree with your new vision, but their heart is still with the way things used to be. So while leading people to new vistas, I have to assure them I will continue to love and nurture them.

That doesn't mean that the pastor has to do the loving and nurturing directly — I can't make every hospital call or attend every graduation party. The challenge, then, is to show people how they can care for each other through strong lay ministry. Qualified deacons and elders can provide hands-on, intimate, person-to-person ministry.

To accomplish that in our setting, we've divided the congregation into "flocks" that elders and deacons nurture and shepherd. They guarantee that the lonely, the sick, the depressed, and the grieving are cared for in a compassionate manner. That gives the pastoral staff the freedom to spend more time beyond the village.

In the final analysis, I want people to know that more is being given to them than is being taken away. Once you've established that, you're on your way toward a new day in the church.

● *Unwelcome visitors.* New ministry attracts new people, and that can be a threat for some longstanding members. They start counting noses and speculate that soon there will be more of "them" than "us." People begin asking themselves quietly, "What will my place be in this new church?"

One way of counteracting parish xenophobia is to assure people that the new changes are going to benefit their children and their grandchildren. I offer the assurance that the church will still be viable two generations from now if we do the right things today. I ask people, "What type of church and world do you want to leave to your grandchildren?" In this disintegrating society, that is a powerful motivator.

● *The parable of the pear trees.* After all is said and done, a leader must sometimes be willing to leave some reluctant followers behind. Jesus did; Paul did. Every generation of church leaders have. That's not the perspective of an ecclesiastical sociopath; that's the reality of leadership.

As much as I would like everyone to follow, sometimes it isn't realistic. Many who aren't willing to follow early on, probably never will. At some point, you have to make a hard decision as to how much time you want to spend in changing reluctant attitudes.

Louis Evans, the former pastor of the National Presbyterian Church for eighteen years, had been leading the church through a long, agonizingly slow process of change. He had just finished a meeting that had gone badly. He went back to his study, slumped in his chair, and looked out his window. The gardener was pruning trees.

He admired this gardener for the way he lovingly and patiently sculptured the trees into globes. Once, though, while the gardener had been in the hospital for heart surgery, some temporary help had changed the shapes of the trees from globes to pears. Louis Evans remembered how the gardener, upon returning to see his trees, turned the air blue with his profanity.

He also remembered something else the gardener said: "It will take years to change the shape of these trees, because you can change the tree only to the degree it has grown."

You can shape a church only to the degree it has grown. For me that means I should invest myself in the process of sculpting new leaders, through discipleship and nurture. Presently I'm trying to spend a year of my life with a small group of men. My plan is for them to go out and spend a year with a similar group of men. Today, by my best estimation, some seventy men in my congregation have been impacted.

● *Staying the course.* Building trust depends on establishing your integrity. And that means staying with something long enough to become believable to people. If I say I'm interested in reaching urban areas with the gospel, I need to hang tough with that dream even if it's not immediately embraced. If I'm still saying the same thing three years from now, people know it's not a passing fad. Doing what you said you were going to do from day one builds trust.

That's a crucial difference between what Leighton Ford calls transformational and transactional leaders. A transactional leader always negotiates his vision, testing its acceptability, watering it down to suit the people. A transformational leader stays with his dream regardless of the storm.

For example, I know a pastor who was having difficulties with a staff member. Her husband was one of his outspoken critics in the church. Finally, he confronted her and said, "This is awkward. But do you feel as negatively toward me as your husband does?" After some hesitation, she said yes. Somewhat stymied as what to do next, he called a friend in the ministry.

After patiently listening to his story, his friend offered some simple advice, "You're the head of staff. If your staff isn't going to be loyal to you, you don't have to work with them. I'd fire her."

He went back and did just that. The husband went ballistic. He was furious at the pastor and insisted he should have "worked it out with her." As my friend said, "I've been hired to lead. It's her job to negotiate her relationship and attitude toward me as her supervisor, not the other way around."

If a church isn't willing to follow my leadership, I don't want to be called the pastor. Call me the facilitator, call me the negotiator or the arbitrator, but don't call me the pastor. Pastors should have the understood right to lead.

The Benefits of Frustration

When the congregation is reluctant to follow, it can hurt. But it can also give one a sense of humility. Our pride and arrogance can deceive us into believing that we have a right to a happy and fulfilling life. But in reality, hardship and suffering are part and parcel of ministry. Just because I have a burning vision doesn't mean I should have an easy road to actualizing it.

I'm reminded of missionaries to India or the Middle East, who might spend an entire lifetime and win only a handful of converts. Is their vision invalid? No; they are just paying the high cost of discipleship.

And when my dreams are stuck in neutral because of congregational reluctance, I'm reminded of the difference between God's eternal purposes in the world and my own limited grasp of what they are. It's more important that I be right about my place in the kingdom of God than insisting on seeing all my dreams be fulfilled. That type of opposition I see as an opportunity for my soul to be cleansed, my focus clarified, and my devotion to serving God renewed.

Controlling information is a process fraught with dangers, but it is vitally important to a ministry characterized by wisdom and integrity.

— *Jack Hayford*

Controlling the Flow of Information

When should a pastor keep a confidence, even at great personal cost to himself or his church?

Several years ago we entered into a purchase agreement to buy a church building and property that also happened to house a private school. The purchase agreement specified that we would assume operation of the school and pledge to keep it open for at least a year and a half, giving the faculty and administration ample time to relocate. We were hoping to begin a school ourselves at some future date, so the agreement appeared to work to everyone's benefit.

The agreement stipulated that once we began making deposits to an escrow account, we were legally and financially in charge of the school's operations. All was going smoothly when disaster struck.

Routine inspections that had accompanied the standard closing procedures revealed a significant amount of asbestos in the school building. The previous owners had known that some asbestos material existed but had no idea of the extent or severity of the problem.

Our church leadership faced a serious dilemma: If we kept our word and opened the school on schedule, as the purchase agreement specified, we would risk endangering the health, and possibly the lives, of school children. If we backed out, citing the potential for high-risk health hazards from the asbestos, we could throw the faculty out of work in mid-August and break our pledge. The projected expense of removing the hazardous material exceeded one million dollars. It looked like a lose-lose situation.

It was an agonizing decision, but we could not in good conscience open the building for a new school year and expose the children to this significant health danger. We decided to slow down the purchase of the school. With the start of school only a few weeks away, the faculty stood between a rock and a hard place. And so did we. To outsiders, it looked as if a good deal had gone bad because we were fickle and untrustworthy.

When our actions were relayed to the school faculty by representatives of the other church, for whatever reason, the asbestos problem was never mentioned. The teachers were simply told the hard realities: we were backing out of the agreement, and they were losing their jobs.

Soon I began receiving scathing letters from disaffected (and unemployed) faculty members. Their correspondence reflected a mixture of confusion and astonishment. Why would a church such as ours, with a reputation for honesty and integrity, suddenly break our word and eliminate their jobs? They were unaware of the asbestos problem, so the only conclusion they could reach was that we lacked basic integrity.

I faced a crucial decision regarding confidentiality and the control of information.

Should I extricate our church from this messy situation by going public with the asbestos problem, and so publicly embarrass the other party? Or should I maintain confidentiality and wait for the other party eventually to explain the whole of the situation? The longer things dragged on, the worse the local press treated us.

I mentally rehearsed how to get out of this dilemma. I could simply call the faculty together and say, "Look folks, let me tell you the whole story. There is a high level of asbestos in this building. We didn't know that when we entered escrow, and apparently neither did your employers. We can't run a school that might cause children health problems now, or even fifteen or twenty years from now. "

Had I done that, I suspect the majority of teachers would have supported our decision. I also suspect that the other church would possibly have been torn within by the anger our unexpected revelations would have produced, with the faculty confronting the church and demanding answers: "Why didn't you tell us about this problem?"

As I said, as if to add insult to injury, we were taking a thrashing in the local press. But whatever temptation I may have felt, it was never a serious option to break our silence and go public.

Instead, I met with the school faculty. I urged each of them to continue to trust our integrity, though circumstances suggested they should do otherwise. "We haven't changed character, though we have been forced to change course," I said. I believe they saw the pain on my face and heard the hurt in my voice. I never mentioned the asbestos problem.

In the following days, we gave each teacher a month's severance pay, though we were under no obligation to do so. God honored our actions in a remarkable fashion. Even though a new school year was nearly underway, every teacher secured a contract in another setting.

All in all, we took a beating at the time, but I'm glad I didn't say anything more than I did.

This situation was extreme, but the issue at stake wasn't all that unusual. Pastors are privy to the secrets of member's lives, secrets that often affect congregational life. We worry about how much to reveal to the entire congregation about individual staff salaries, or how much detail we should report to the church regarding a dishonest building contractor. Church leaders fail morally, and we wrestle with how specific to be with the congregation.

Sometimes these situations seem insoluble.

As we consider the control of information, what hazards should we be aware of? What information should we divulge and what should we restrict? How do we handle the pressure personally?

Many Dangers, Toils, and Snares

Controlling information is a process fraught with dangers, but it is vitally important to a ministry characterized by wisdom and integrity.

The first danger of secrecy is it tends to carry in it the seeds of pride and power. I can control others by choosing what I will and will not tell them. If I know the board is going to cut one of two staff members, I could play them off one another: in separate conversations, I could see which one would be more willing to take a pay cut or shoulder more responsibilities — and then encourage the board to let the other one go.

Another destructive side of secrecy occurs when you are privy to information long before anyone else. As a public announcement is being made regarding a matter you knew about long ago, it's tempting to sit back and think, *I'm way ahead of everyone else. I'm important.* It gives you a temporary sense of significance, but something devious is happening in your soul. Pride is seeping into the deep wells of your personality.

Or I can manipulate people and wield extraordinary power by leading individuals to believe I'm sharing privileged information with only them. I simply have to call in one staff member and say, "Bill, I think so highly of you, let me tell you what's happening with . . ." and then drop the juicy tidbit. Then I could call in the next staff member and say essentially the same thing, assuring each person he or she is favored, creating a sense of loyalty based on a lying manipulation. That is evil.

Not all secrets are evil in and of themselves. Some are simply points of privacy, such as those that exist between a husband and wife. Even though our family is open, we don't tell our children everything. The dynamics of intimacy and deep relationships require some holding back.

The key is to search my own motives. Am I controlling information for the purpose of controlling people, or am I withholding information for the purpose of serving their best interests?

In guarding against the sinister use of secrets, I make sure I use no intrigues. If I share something with one member of the executive team, I share it with all the members of the team. That way, there are no hidden intrigues to divide the group.

For example, I once was faced with a decision as to how much to tell the staff when a particular staff member resigned in anger.

When this man first submitted his resignation, I called him in and said, "I'm not going to accept your resignation. That doesn't mean you can't resign, but I'm not going to accept your letter at this time. I'd like you to think it over for a few more days." He looked bewildered but agreed to follow my advice. A few days later I received a letter in which he reaffirmed his decision to leave.

This time I honored his wishes, and we set a date for severance. But just a week before he was to conclude his ministry with us, he unexpectedly withdrew his letter. The family circumstance that initiated his resignation had changed, so he reverted to my earlier offer to reject his resignation.

Yet, just six weeks later, he *again* gave notice he was resigning. He was disappointed that we did not dismiss the person we trained to take over his position. Even though we tried to work out an amenable integration of the two positions, he was unhappy, feeling somehow diminished (even though we had not demoted him). Now he was leaving, and not without bitterness toward the church, and I guessed sooner or later people would question why he left.

Our executive pastoral team (7 persons) is responsible for the overall flow of information in the church. We wrestled with the question of how much to tell the rest of the pastoral staff (20 additional persons) about his reasons for resigning.

We opted for sharing the facts with the whole pastoral team not to defend ourselves but to avoid confusion. We explained the person's reasons for leaving, being sure to be forthright but gentle. I asked the pastoral team to hold this confidence, yet I was as candid as possible regarding the man's disappointment with the church. It helped lay the matter to rest.

I also try to develop a staff mind set. When I ask staff members to keep a confidence, I'm not being secretive. We're no clandestine cult where only the "initiated" know the inner workings of the group. Nor do I believe that the congregation is "too dumb" to be trusted with sensitive information.

Rather, I want my staff to see information as a trust, and they understand we limit it to reflect the wisdom and gentleness of Christ in dealing with others. My basic concern is to serve people's best interest.

A staff member sometimes will understandably ask , "May I share this with my spouse?" I never ask staff to withhold information from spouses. I have a high view of the oneness and sanctity of marriage. If a spouse volunteers to be exempted from hearing matters of confidentiality, that's his or her choice. If they decide as a couple not to burden each other with certain matters, that's fine. But I will never request — nor would I foolishly attempt to compel them to keep secrets from each other.

These two simple, common-sense steps work to detoxify secretiveness in a staff setting. I believe they also work to create trust and integrity.

A Matter of Degrees and Timing

When do I share privileged information or decide to restrict it? When does a church member have a "right to know" sensitive or potentially embarrassing information? Whose permission do I need to go public?

In my twenty-three years of ministry in my present church, I have encountered two episodes of serious moral failure involving staff. In both cases we controlled the flow of information until we were ready to relate the appropriate facts in sequence to the appropriate levels of church leadership.

In the first case, we waited nearly eight days until we were ready to share the tragic news with the congregation. Why the delay? We wanted to protect both the person involved and the congregation from unnecessary harm. Pacing was crucial to assure avoidance of dumping the failure on the body.

Through careful steps we provided differing levels of confidence, according to a person's responsibility in the church. The few who needed to know all the sorry details were told everything. Those who needed to know only the basic outline of the incident learned nothing more than that. We meticulously worked through the process so that by the time we informed the congregation, over two hundred leaders had been informed. We told the congregation that specific sexual immorality was the problem, and the offending pastor confessed it of his own volition. But the details were not elaborated.

There was another case, a report of indiscretions by a staff pastor that stopped short of complete moral failure. In this case, the staff member made a veiled proposition to a woman in the church.

It came to light in an executive staff meeting through a report brought by the offended woman. When the pastoral staff member was brought before three of our executive team, he denied the charges, and then a supernatural thing happened.

Our lead administrator turned to the guilty but unconfessing pastor and said, "You're not telling us about the day you were sitting in a car with another woman." Our administrator specifically described the location of their meeting, the content of their conversation, and the color of the woman's clothing. Since the administrator had no prior knowledge of the incident, I concluded that the Holy Spirit had revealed the information to him. The guilty staff member literally collapsed and tearfully confessed his sin.

This was an awkward situation, yet we neither removed the pastor nor informed the congregation, but we did bring him under strong discipline. We were able to deal with the problem before his weakness led to a total moral failure.

We were able to correct another situation before it reached the general congregation. Our church ethos encourages hugging one another. Several people noticed that the embrace between one of our leaders and a woman in the congregation often seemed intimate rather than brotherly-sisterly. When it was brought to our attention, we informed only the executive, one elder and his wife, and we confronted the pastor privately. Why? Because the pastor hugging the woman had not yet crossed a line of transgression requiring public rebuke. Both love and wisdom demanded in this case we protect his reputation and guard his ability to minister in the future. Love covers a multitude of sins.

Does that imply we should hide transgressions? No. Love never glosses over sin. Love doesn't sweep things under the rug. My congregation will attest that when something demands public disclosure, we lead toward that in an open yet gracious way.

Controlling information in many cases is an act of love. "Covering" people in that case is not the same as a cover-up, but an act of nurture and protection.

The Truth about Finances

Financial information is a particularly delicate area to talk about publicly. Here's how we deal with two such issues.

● *Salaries.* Do church members have the right to know anything they wish about the operation of the church, including individual staff salaries? Does their giving to the church imply an ownership granting them free access to any and all information?

My answer to both questions is no.

Not everyone wants to know the yearly salaries of individual staff members. It's silly to force information on people who don't care to know what the youth pastor earns.

Rather than share salary information in a shotgun fashion, I use a need-to-know test with two parts. First, do people need to know this information because the staff member's salary is raising serious questions? Second, is this information pertinent to a leadership issue and being requested by an appropriately positioned leader in the church? If individuals meet either of these two criteria, I will consider sharing privileged salary information.

Generally, though, there's no compelling need or right for people to know how much a pastor takes home each month. First, in the workplace this is private information, and the church should be at least as courteous. Second, many people cannot appreciate the various considerations that went into his final package. Thus, I opt to keep the information confidential (and I'm supported by our church elders in doing so).

The average median income in our city for a family of four is approximately $35,000 per year. Naturally, many in our congregation make somewhat less. The church pastoral staff, however, is composed of highly trained, capable, and qualified professionals, and their remuneration reflects it.

Individual salaries made a matter of public record could easily provoke envy or bitterness. Few would argue they don't deserve their salaries, but those making significantly less could be tempted toward jealousy. To avoid that and other problems, we lump salary figures in one budget item in reporting.

When I report that figure at our annual business meeting, I often do so light-heartedly: "I'm sure all of you noticed that the staff salary line item exceeds a million and a half dollars this year. Half of that is my salary alone!"

Once the laughter subsides, I explain, "Though the figure looks enormous at first glance, keep in mind it supports over 100 families." I then detail the salary components, including our medical, dental, retirement, and other benefits. Once people understand the various costs, they agree our salaries are equitable.

I did on one occasion, however, reveal my own salary figure to a sizable but select group within the congregation. It was during the televangelist scandals of the late 1980s. To ensure people of my integrity, I felt at least a few key people should know what I earned.

I scheduled a series of back yard desserts at the parsonage. We invited about thirty people at a time (a total of 300), selecting these people based on how they served in the body and how vital it was they have full confidence in our financial dealings. They hadn't had doubts, but they were greatly reassured.

On one other occasion, we made pastoral staff salaries a public matter. During the depths of a recession, our pastoral team asked not to receive a salary increase that year, expressing a concern for many in the church who were losing jobs. I shared that piece of information from the pulpit during a morning sermon. You could just feel the appreciation of the people. It confirmed in their minds the shepherding, servant spirit of these men and women, and that the pastors existed to serve, not exploit the church.

In no other business does everyone know what everyone else is paid. Why, then, require church staff to divulge something so intensely personal? Justice, equity, and fairness demands that church employees receive the same considerations members of the congregation enjoy.

● *Financial records.* When an individual in the congregation *demands* access to financial records but has no basis for an accusation of mismanagement of funds, I know I'm facing a spiritual, and not managerial, battle. In such cases, the inquiry is not usually a quest to affirm integrity but to gain control.

I keep such unreasonable requests to a minimum by focusing on the basics. I occasionally remind the congregation that the Holy Spirit controls the church, not any one person or group of people — and certainly not me. I reiterate that we conduct our affairs on a biblical model of conferred authority. When the church elects deacons and leaders, the people authorize them to use their office to distribute funds as best they see fit.

That doesn't mean individuals can't raise legitimate questions. We have an open-door policy.

"Never feel that asking a question insinuates you lack trust in the leadership," I assure our members. "In fact, you may ask any question you wish of our financial administrator or other staff members." At most three or four people take us up on that invitation in a year, and they are received with courtesy and trust. Almost always they inquire not out of doubt but out of a desire to investigate ways to help.

The Loneliness of Keeping a Confidence

As I mentioned at the beginning of the chapter, withholding information out of a sense of integrity can exact a high price. We will be misunderstood and misrepresented. During the crisis of closing the school, about a hundred of our people seemed to "evaporate" by starting to attend one of our "daughter" churches.

Watching that exodus cut deeply into my soul. Though few ever said so directly, I knew they questioned our fidelity. They were bewildered. (Sheep are easily scattered when a shepherd can't raise his voice.)

Only my wife knew the deep valley I passed through during those days. Alone, I agonized; I prayed; I wept.

During the darkest of those days, the Lord did a remarkable work in my life. He gave me a dream one evening that began to restore my peace of mind. Then, while I was reading the Psalms one night, a portion of Scripture came alive in such a powerful way I suddenly sat up wide-eyed. I couldn't stop reading. With tears in my eyes I sensed the Holy Spirit saying, "I'm going to take care of this. It's all going to work out." My unanswered questions dissolved in the seas of his assurance and presence.

The asbestos eventually was removed from the building, and we completed the purchase. We did not have to jeopardize the rights and reputation of either congregation.

The other pastor later thanked me for our conduct during the crisis. Almost two years later, word about what really happened leaked out little by little. I received several apologies from those who had misjudged us. I learned that God honors integrity, even when it hurts.

Though it was painful, we had done the right thing.

Lonely as keeping a confidence may be, I learned a valuable lesson. When God calls us to control information in the best interest of others, he can also be trusted to control the situation.

Leading a church during its zenith, like coaching a successful basketball team, is an odyssey, an adventurous combination of pain and joy.

— Leith Anderson

Chapter Seven

When Everything Is Going Right

Recently a pastor flew to Minneapolis just to meet with me for two hours. Near the end of our conversation, he asked, "What is it like to be successful?"

His question caught me by surprise, because I, like most pastors, live with the day-to-day reality of local church ministry: I don't think of myself as successful.

In 1992, after the Chicago Bulls had won their second straight NBA championship, head coach Phil Jackson was asked about the difference between the first championship season and the second.

"Last year it was a honeymoon," said Jackson. "This year it was an odyssey."

The ecstasy of coaching the Bulls' first championship had been followed by the anguish of leading them to repeat their success. The Bulls' squad, led by Michael Jordan, was essentially intact from the previous season. But their burning passion to win, which they had their first championship season, was noticeably absent at times. In addition, every team was gunning for them. In the playoffs, their opponents sometimes came from behind to beat the Bulls. They almost lost a second championship.

As I reflected on my friend's question, I realized success from the outside looks great — a growing megachurch with staff, programs, and financial resources. From the inside, though, it feels like an odyssey, with moments of joy attended with many pressures — staff issues, performance pressures, periods of heavy debt.

Leading when everything is going right is just as challenging as leading when everything is going wrong. During good times I try to be on top of things with the same intensity so that I can meet the challenges and take advantage of unique opportunities.

The Golden Handcuffs

In some ways, success *is* all it's cracked up to be. Leading in good times, like surfing the perfect wave, is a thrill. Though it has its pressures, I'll take it any day over failure.

In the shoot-'em-up TV show "The A-Team," Hannibal Smith, the motley squad's leader, would occasionally pull his cigar out of his mouth — while bullets flew and the bad guys were winning — and growl, "I love it when a plan comes together."

As the church's pastor, I too love it when a plan comes together, when broken people go from disaster to healing to helping others. After sixteen years at Wooddale, I've had the enormous satisfaction of seeing God's plan realized in this ministry.

Through our ministry a woman came to faith in Christ. Her skeptical husband, after finally coming to church one Sunday, was upset with me. He didn't like what his wife had become. I met with both of them for four hours one evening, attempting to answer his questions like, "Is there a God?" and "Is there absolute truth?"

Impressed by my patience to discuss his questions, he returned to church the following Sunday. Later he became a follower of Christ, and recently, both of them told their faith stories in a Sunday service. Now they're zealously seeking to win their family and friends to Christ.

That's addicting. But there's more.

Years ago, I heard Billy Graham speak at an Urbana missions conference. Though the other speakers that week spoke eloquently and deeply, clearly the crowd's accolades went to Graham.

His talk, frankly, wasn't any better than the rest of that week's lineup. The audience, though, respected Graham's accumulated credibility from his lifetime of integrity and faithfulness. They ascribed to his Urbana sermon an excellence even beyond its high quality.

In that sense, success relieves some of the constant pressure to prove oneself. And that's nice. If I consistently preach good sermons, the congregation will grow accustomed to excellence. So when I do have an off Sunday, they'll give me the benefit of the doubt. That relieves a lot of pressure.

Good times also enhance your credibility. If an army general has won ten battles in a row, the top brass will want him in command. If a baseball pitcher has a history of weathering stormy innings, especially with bases loaded and no outs, the manager will want him on the mound. So will congregations want successful pastors.

As I've mentioned, while Wooddale was building its new worship center, I asked the leadership to plant a church in the Minneapolis area. To do so meant diverting financial and people resources and possibly jeopardizing our building project. The church voted to step out in faith.

Past successes gave me credibility to make a solid case for the church start. I might not have been able to lead in that direction had the church not been growing.

Bursting the Bubble

Pastors of successful churches quickly discover that the grass is not necessarily greener on the "success" side of the fence. While leading during good times, I've discovered two popular, though bogus, notions about success.

• *Ministry is easier.* From a distance, successful ministries are often idealized. Successful pastors sometimes perpetuate this by exporting their successes in church growth seminars across the country. It's somewhat akin to the bucolic, medieval Camelot in which King Arthur lived. From the outside, King Arthur had the perfect job in a perfect world. The turmoil inside Camelot, however, eventually brought down the knights of the Round Table.

At Wooddale, we have a futures task force that has been hard at work creating a long-term dream for the church. The task force met with Wooddale's elder board to present this "dream for the next decade," which involved, among other things, changing our purpose and organizational structure — a critical piece of legislation.

That evening, the discussion about Wooddale's future got sidetracked. Instead of igniting passion for what God might do, the meeting drifted into a discussion about our current Sunday evening service.

Even after Wooddale's successes, motivating still takes hard work. I'm still amazed that I can give a seminar about how to change an inward-looking church into an evangelistic church and then return to Minneapolis only to find I can't get a bulletin board changed. Success doesn't change the day-to-day reality of parish ministry.

• *Pastors are the single cause for success.* At seminars or pastors' conferences, often I'm asked, "How did you ever get Wooddale's leadership to the point where they are? How did you train them to think strategically?"

The question assumes that I was responsible for nurturing great leadership. Wooddale could boast of excellent leadership long before I arrived. I'm the beneficiary of the successes and skills of a host of other people. (Maybe that's one reason why I'm reluctant to leave. If I go elsewhere and don't succeed, people will know I wasn't the reason at Wooddale!)

A pastor I know with a successful ministry recently moved to another part of the country. Nearing retirement, he had decided to take on a difficult parish, as he had thirty-five years earlier. This time, though, he failed, and he was surprised and disappointed. He assumed that his success could be exported to another time and place. But the chemistry just wasn't there.

Success is complex. In addition to the Holy Spirit, a host of factors contribute to an organization's success or failure — timing, the culture, the pastor, the staff. Too often in church work, God gets the glory if it succeeds, and we pastors get the blame if it fails. God should always get the glory, but pastors shouldn't necessarily assume all the blame.

Plowing a Straight Furrow

When things are going well — steady numerical and spiritual growth, financial solvency, and an infectious enthusiasm about God's presence — leaders will encounter subtle shifts towards entropy.

For instance, subtle pride can creep in. There's no therapy group for successful church leaders, no place where pastors can go and say, "Things are really going great. Please uphold me in prayer and hold me accountable." Sometimes I think there ought to be such a place, for ministry success is dangerous.

I had lunch with a friend who pastors a local Presbyterian church. In the weeks following Easter, he ran into several other pastors, asking how their Easter services went.

"Every pastor quoted the number of people who attended their services," my friend said. "Not one mentioned Jesus Christ or having an experience with God."

Pride of this sort is a subtle sin that takes some strange expressions. Typically, it is stereotyped as: "I'm wonderful. I do everything well. I'm the best there is." More subtly it says, "I feel so blessed that the Lord is using me in such great ways."

My struggle is with a reverse pride: I'm not as tempted toward arrogance as I am with discouragement when everything doesn't go as I had hoped. I become too bothered with circumstances and programs not being the way *I* want them to be.

What I am really saying is "I'm the most important person in this ministry. I've got to have it my way, and if it's not my way, it's wrong." This is egocentric, and something I want to avoid.

Connected closely with pride is the narcotic of approval, which can drug us during periods of success.

I find myself falling into typically human patterns. If I'm not congratulated on how well I've done, I'll ask someone for a "critique," knowing full well I'm likely to get some strokes. If I've been criticized, I run to others, asking for their opinion, telling them how I've been criticized. I know who most likely will affirm me as a good preacher or Bible teacher or leader or administrator. Like most people, I'm insecure at times. Ironically, success can sometimes make me more insecure and in need of approval.

Part of that is due to rising standards. When Roger Bannister broke the four-minute mile barrier, the world standard for running a mile was changed. Today, however, Bannister wouldn't even qualify for the Olympics.

Success raises the standards. This year's Easter service needs to top last year's. This is reinforced by the way we pastors fudge on the number of people who attend our church. I've never met a pastor, including myself, who rounds *down* to a lower hundred — 377 is not "about 350" but "about 400," 1,420 is not 1,400 but "nearly 1,500."

In today's culture, the bar for pastors has been set at world-record height. However, not everyone will be able to pole vault nineteen feet. Not everyone can win a gold. Likewise, every pastor will not pastor a church that easily fulfills its mission and relates to its community and grows into a megachurch.

The baby boomer generation is clearly motivated by success, which is an added pressure to modern pastors. Pre-World War II generations were motivated more by hardship. Fund-raising letters are an example of this.

The previous generation responds well to a letter crying, "If we don't receive $50,000 before December 31, we might have to shut our doors." "Boomers" are less willing to throw good money after bad. They like to jump on the bandwagon of success — "We reached 4,000 youth last summer. With your help, we can reach even more this summer." That's one reason boomers flock to megachurches.

Much of the pressure to succeed is internal. I tend to pick the external pressures that correspond with my own internal expectations. If I'm insecure about who I am, I might become a workaholic, believing that I'll be successful only when I pastor a large congregation. I then imagine the congregation expects the church to grow 15 percent each year. In fact, the expectation originates with my own psychological weaknesses.

Often, when pastors burn out and then reveal to their congregations the pressure they've been under, their congregations are shocked. They say, "I thought he was doing fine. Everything appeared to be going so well."

When leading in good times, often the inward desire to continue our success can victimize — and potentially sabotage — God's blessing in our ministry.

Finally, there is the fear of incompetence. I've been told that no one who has won a Nobel Prize has made a significant contribution to science or literature thereafter. The achievement curtails itself from being repeated. The effort to win the first Nobel Prize saps too much from the individual. That can feel threatening to the successful pastor. Success can limit success.

Each of us has only so much giftedness and energy. We may be able to lead a church to only a certain level of success. And then we simply can't run any faster. *What if I don't have any more to give?* I've wondered. *What if I don't have any way to do better next time?* More success means a higher standard, and at some point, I might not be competent to lead the church.

I also wonder about getting older. At age 48, I still feel up to the task of leading this church. But what about when I'm 55? Is church growth a young man's game? What if I don't have the personal resources to succeed with ten years until retirement?

These fears aren't crippling, and in my normal routine I'm not too concerned about such issues. I don't have to be a Nobel Prize-winning leader to lead a church effectively. Still, I'm wise to monitor such emotions to make sure I don't get prematurely discouraged or fall into patterns that would undermine the gifts and abilities I do have.

Recession Proofing Your Ministry

I want to be at my best when God expands his economy in Wooddale Church. God is in the success business — isn't the kingdom of God about expansion and growth? So I try to be focused when in the midst of his blessing.

● *Service your networks.* My wife, Charleen, and I invited to our home a local pastor whom I've known since ninth grade. We attended high school together and then went our separate ways for twenty years.

Now that we live in the same area, we've been able to renew our old friendship. We've talked about plans to drive a minivan to New Jersey for our high school reunion. Whether we actually attend the reunion is irrelevant to the time we could spend together driving there and back.

Pursuing and developing our friendship is important to me. Success heightens the need for close relationships because of its pull toward isolation. Many of my friends are forthright with me, helping me cut through the self-deceit success can bring.

My friends help me keep success in perspective. My world is relatively small; my successes are small. A network of close relationships keeps my feet on the ground. Servicing that network is important especially when things are going well.

● *Allow others to succeed.* As a teenager, I always made sure I got in my share of waterskiing — and even a few extra shares. I loved the sport. I'd do anything for a turn on the water.

Today, I'd rather watch my own kids ski. They are far better than I ever was — they slalom, barefoot, and perform acrobatics I never dared to do. Driving the boat isn't even important to me. I just enjoy watching them excel for the pure, simple pleasure of seeing them succeed.

The same is true in ministry. I get a great satisfaction sitting in a worship service and hearing a young pastor preach a good sermon. Much of the satisfaction comes from feeling that I had a part in his success. I'm involved in growing successful people, not just an institution. And that helps me focus on people rather than things, on others rather than myself.

● *Realign self.* With the busyness and demands of success comes the need for a reality check, to realign oneself with what is and what should never be. It is separating myself from the enterprise.

Pastors have a hard time distinguishing between who we are and what we do. A person of integrity, of wholeness, stops periodically and says, "How do who-I-am and what-I-do fit together?"

Charleen and I own a lake cabin in northern Minnesota, where I can go and not be a pastor, where I won't run into many parishioners. I'm just me. I'm just an average guy who wears jeans and a sweatshirt, like everyone else.

On the lake, I can clear my head and ask myself, *How does this part of me fit with the pastoral part? How does what I say publicly fit with what I do privately?* To me, it would be awful to appear different publicly than I am privately. I either adjust what I'm saying or adjust who I am. A continual process of realignment helps me do just that.

● *Reach outward.* A pastor of a large church was having some problems in his congregation. I didn't know him well, but I felt compelled to see if I could help. I called the church office.

"He's not taking calls," the secretary said. "The church gave him a leave of absence. He's out of town."

"Well, just leave a note with my office and home number," I replied. "He doesn't need to call me back, but if he wants to talk, I'd be glad to talk with him."

He returned my call. Later I discovered I was the only person who had called him — not his denomination, not other staff members, nor other pastors. That experience has reaffirmed my desire to look outward in the good times, taking the initiative to help others.

● *Get a Merlin mentor.* I believe everyone should have a mentor, especially younger pastors. After being damaged by something or someone, a mentor can say, "Oh yeah, I know all about that. That's happened to me a lot of times." Suddenly, I'm okay. I'm going to make it through my down time.

This mentor doesn't have to be alive or even know that he or she is a mentor. In one scene in the movie *Camelot*, with the unanimity and integrity of the Round Table falling apart, King Arthur is desperate: Lady Guinnevere is having an affair with Lancelot, and the other knights are fighting among themselves.

What does King Arthur do? He walks into the forest and reflects, *What would Merlin do?* Merlin, by this time, was dead. Still, he mentored the king from the past. King Arthur placed himself in Merlin's shoes and thought about his problems from Merlin's perspective.

Like Merlin to King Arthur, Harry Emerson Fosdick has been my mentor from the past. Fosdick pastored a church in New Jersey, close to where I grew up. I've read his biography and listened to his sermons on tape. While I disagree with his theology, Fosdick has mentored me through his view that preaching is counseling. He's had a profound influence on my ministry.

All pastors should pick mentors. We can't figure out everything for ourselves. We need the wisdom and comfort of others to navigate the waters of ministry. Choosing mentors — alive or otherwise — is a powerful tool to monitor our emotions and guide our decisions during the roller coaster of ministry success.

● *Find what restores you.* Discouragement often sets in after success — mostly because we're emotionally and physically depleted. So I've tried to restore my energies regularly.

Throughout my entire ministry, I've worked on Mondays. I've never taken it off. In fact, everybody at Wooddale works on Monday; that's when our staff meets. Often we're tired and on the emotional downside of a successful Sunday. But by being together, we find encouragement and strength.

If I stayed home and slept on Mondays, I'd compound my

discouragement. It would run like a virus through my emotions. (I also have a theory about days off: if I'm going to be depressed and thinking about resigning, I would rather be paid for that day than waste it at home!)

It's Not Over Till It's Over

When I was in the seventh grade, my father, who rarely took me to sporting events, said, "I've got a couple of tickets to the World Series today. How about going with me?"

I was excited. I'd never been to a major league baseball game. So my father and I drove to New York from our home in New Jersey and went to the game. I was a Brooklyn Dodger fan, but that afternoon, no Brooklyn Dodger even got to first base. They were shut out. I went home, crushed.

Not until twenty years later did I realize what I had witnessed. What I thought was defeat — my favorite team had gotten sorely beaten — was an astonishing historic moment of victory: Don Larson of the New York Yankees pitched the only perfect game ever in World Series history.

Often what is perceived as failure or success does not correspond to our reality. In the end, only God knows. But during those times when success seems apparent, I've learned to relish its benefits and pay close attention to its effect on my soul and my ministry.

Strong leaders are known for their landmark sermons.
— Jack Hayford

CHAPTER EIGHT

Preaching the Landmark Sermon

Whatever a pastor's position on wine drinking, it's not hard to marshal proof texts. I believe a case can be made either way. Although it's a controversial subject, several years ago I needed to deal directly with the subject with our Servants Council, a group of several hundred key people in our congregation.

As I wrestled with the issue in my study, I felt the internal pressure of being responsible for these leaders and their influence on our whole congregation. They needed a shepherd-like spirit instilled in them for rightly guiding all whom they taught and touched. This had to be explained in a loving way, rather than legalistically. My heart whispered, *You better help them see this clearly. Most of our people are going to decide what's right and wrong based on what you say and how you act.*

I also was concerned with external pressure, about the larger Christian community, that others might pass judgment on me. I could hear some saying, "Hayford is soft on drinking" (for not out-of-hand declaring a teetotaling stance) or "Hayford is a legalist" (because I concerned myself with the issue).

Strong leaders are known for their landmark sermons (and sometimes lynched for them). Landmark sermons are the defining moments of a church and a pastor. Without them there are no boundaries, no rallying points, no banners in the sand; there is nothing to communicate vision and goals, policies and practices, beliefs and standards.

Like Joshua's landmark recitation of the law with its blessings and curses at Mount Ebal, landmark sermons are memorable, weighty, conclusive, directive, never inconspicuous. After hearing them, the congregation feels that a line has been drawn in the sand — or in stone.

Some will regard your landmark sermon as a familiar "oak tree" on the church landscape, guiding them in the way they should go; others, deeming the sermon a garish neon sign, will wish it didn't mark the land. But no one can ignore such sermons or their consequences.

What classifies as a landmark sermon? How can we make them more effective? When should they be given?

The Purposes of Landmark Sermons

Landmark sermons are highly visible for good reason. They tower above the normal weekly sermon because they accomplish at least one of six purposes.

1. To address questions that weigh on people's consciences. Ethical and theological questions bear heavily on many people.

Dozens of women who have had an abortion have committed

their lives to Christ in our church, for instance. Sooner or later most accept God's forgiveness, but they wonder, *If that really was a person who was aborted, where is he or she now?* Their guilt and concern can be unbearable. Those who have suffered a miscarriage can raise the same question.

After counseling several women, I decided to preach a sermon on what happens to the soul of an aborted child. In a message titled, "Short-Circuited Into Eternity," I took a clear sanctity-of-life stance but was not condemning. I made it clear that the child had not reached an age of accountability and thus was innocent in God's sight.

Many Christians worry in silence about other troubling issues: Have I committed the unforgivable sin? Will God forgive my divorce and remarriage? Can a "backslider" be forgiven? What if my job requires me to work on Sunday? Preaching on such subjects can clearly guide people through their confusion.

2. To prepare the congregation for a church project. As I describe in chapter two, several years ago we purchased an $11 million church complex as a second facility. Before I proposed this move, I preached for ten weeks in the Book of Joshua on the subject "Possess Your Tomorrows." The main idea of this series — God promises us many things, but we have to move in and "possess" them — became part of the spiritual rationale for buying the property. Of course, it also encouraged individuals to "possess" what God had ordained for them.

Whether it's building a church, beginning more children's ministries, or launching small groups, people in the congregation need the motivation, insight, and challenge that can come only from their pastor's sermons.

3. To put landmark moments in biblical perspective. When the big earthquake hit San Francisco in 1989, I heard some say God was judging the homosexual community of that city. Landmark moments beg for landmark sermons, whether the issue is God's judgment, end-times prophecy, or the morality of war.

The week after the San Francisco earthquake, I chose as my text Christ's comment on two tragedies: the collapsing tower that killed eighteen and Pilate's mixing some of his victims' blood with their sacrifices. The consensus was that these victims were more sinful than others. But Jesus refuted the conventional wisdom.

My sermon's main point was "If God is judging San Francisco, we all better dive under our chairs right now." I acknowledged that while such a catastrophe *could* be an expression of God's judgment, it is a mistake to conclude it happened because some people are more deserving of judgment than others.

Although I had expressed many of that sermon's ideas in bits and pieces before, the landmark moment made it a landmark message.

4. *To change policies.* Over time, a church may shift or evolve in regard to membership policies, leadership qualifications, whom to marry or bury or baptize, to whom to serve the sacraments, lifestyle, and nonessential doctrinal matters. Such controversial topics beckon for a landmark sermon or series of sermons.

In the early 1970s, the predominant stance in my tradition had been that all divorced persons were unmarriageable on biblical grounds. Wrestling with the whole truth of the Scriptures, being driven there by tough questions that were raised in my soul as I talked with broken people, I came to a different conclusion: that persons divorced prior to their decision to follow Christ were eligible for marriage on the grounds that their past was forgiven and forgotten by God.

I preached a sermon on the subject on a Sunday night and concluded the message by performing the wedding of a couple who had each been divorced under those conditions. (Our policy, though, is not simplistic or arbitrary: there are specific stipulations governing how each situation is handled.)

5. *To confront cultural trends.* A year after the PTL scandal and five weeks after Jimmy Swaggart's problems came to light, I decided to preach a sermon on restoring fallen leaders. I had heard so many advocate that because God forgives a fallen leader, his sins should not disallow him from continuing in ministry, that if he repented, he could continue in leadership without a period of probation. I challenged that.

In my sermon I made what I feel is a biblical distinction: God forgives us instantly, but being forgiven isn't the only qualification for Christian leadership. Being forgiven isn't the same thing as rectifying character. Scripture says that potential leaders must be tested and proven over time to see whether certain essential qualities are present in their lives. I concluded that a leader who violates the qualifications of leadership must again be proven and tested over time before being restored to a position in the church.

6. *To bring healing at times of human failure.* When key members fall short of biblical morality, it shakes the church. Several years ago the daughter of one of our elders gave birth to a child out of wedlock. Later, when the issue of her immorality had been resolved, she asked for the child to be dedicated in church. We did so on a Sunday night. I preached a sermon on justice and mercy, asserting that we are obligated to stand on the side of mercy even when we run the risk of appearing to have sacrificed righteousness.

I concluded that sermon by calling the girl and her child forward, and the congregation joined me in dedicating this child to the Lord. No one felt standards had been sacrificed, and everyone recognized God's mercy was being manifest.

I also called to the platform the baby's grandfather, our elder. "John (not his real name) has submitted to the board his resignation as an elder," I announced. "We did not ask for his resignation, but he knew that at this time his family required his special attention, and so he did the right thing in submitting it."

There wasn't a dry eye in the place.

Mistakes to Avoid

Landmark sermons have their own special temptations. Here are some mistakes I try to avoid.

● *Sensationalism or exploitation.* When the news first broke about Magic Johnson having the HIV virus, I considered preaching on sexual morality. The more I thought about it, though, the less I liked the idea.

It was a judgment call; many ministers did preach on it, of

course, and I may have missed a landmark moment. But especially since I serve in the Los Angeles area, I felt I would be sensationalizing the subject or capitalizing on someone else's tragedy.

To test whether I'm tempted to sensationalize a theme, I ask myself these questions:

1. Am I concerned with this theme mainly to draw a crowd or to truly edify the flock?

2. Am I dealing with it substantively and biblically, or merely "grabbing a topic" and then glossing over the problem and only giving a superficial "lick and a promise" with a quick verse or two?

3. Is the issue crucial to the moment? Can I wait — should I wait — until a more profitable moment?

● *Giving the message to the wrong group.* Some messages are suited for smaller circles within the church because of the differences between followers and leaders, males and females, children and adults, new Christians and mature Christians, the young and the old, the committed and the peripheral. What will be a landmark for a small group in the church may be irrelevant or confusing to some of the Sunday-morning-only attenders.

I did, in fact, deliver a message at the time of the Magic Johnson incident but only to our men's group. I felt the message was more appropriate there.

● *Imbalance.* When I spoke to our leaders on the subject of wine drinking, I showed them the Scriptures that support both sides of the issue, but then I took my position: "I can't make a biblical case against wine drinking, but I feel this is one of those rare times when the Bible has a double standard for leaders and followers. That is why, personally, I have made a commitment never to drink alcoholic beverages of any kind."

I'm always concerned about touching all the bases and have found that people respond to that. Several of the elders in our church are attorneys, and some have specifically commented, "Pastor, I appreciate the way you cover all sides of these controversial issues. I feel we can make valid decisions because the whole case is presented." A balanced message shows respect for people's intelligence and confidence in their spiritual decision-making abilities.

This doesn't mean I don't draw a conclusive point, but I do speak with respect toward positions I oppose.

Keys to Effectiveness

I have a strong sense of anointing as I prepare and deliver landmark sermons. I sense that these messages are more than simply teachings or exhortations; they're prophetic. I'm presenting the counsel of God conclusively and categorically on a critical issue.

Still, I recognize the human dimension. Many factors can make people more or less receptive to what I'm going to say. Here are some of the things I do to make my landmark sermons more effective.

● *Maintain the tensions.* Our tendency is to try to resolve the dynamic tension of truth, to oversimplify or go to extremes, but I have found that the truth is found in tension.

Ten years ago one member of our singles group worship team had a recurring problem with severe depression. He took medication to counteract it, but at times he would neglect his prescription and the chemical imbalance would bring terrible suffering. At one such time he took his life — jumping off a building near downtown.

Although only a fraction of the congregation knew him, he was a significant leader to enough singles that I felt I had to address the subject of suicide.

In my sermon, I emphasized the comforting grounds of our salvation — the grace of God and the death of Christ — but I also stressed our moral responsibility as stewards of God's gift of life. Such tensions may make landmark sermons controversial — but they also become inescapably confrontational and memorable.

● *Point to the overarching principles of Scripture.* Universal principles are crucial to every decision, question, or problem that landmark sermons address. My job is to find the big picture in a particular situation, for overarching principles provide the deepest insights and broadest perspectives.

In 1990 and '91, as the Persian Gulf crisis dominated the headlines, I preached on such issues as, "Does God Desire War?"

"How Patriotic Should I Be When My Country Is at War?" "What Is My Christian Responsibility During a War?" I can't answer big questions about war without touching on great themes: how God views the nations, especially Israel, and how God views secular authority. Landmarks are built with huge stones and deep foundations.

● *Take adequate time.* There are no landmark sermonettes. My landmark sermons take an hour to an hour and fifteen minutes to deliver (I usually give them on Sunday night). When I'm preaching a definitive word, I can't be sloppy or shallow, and I can't be brief, superficial, or simplistic. I take pains to exegete Scripture, select and define terms, frame the big questions, and focus the issue. I distinguish carefully between what I do — and don't — mean.

While preaching through a five-installment overview of the Book of Ezekiel on Sunday nights, I decided to spend an entire sermon on chapter 18 (fathers and children should be punished for their own sins, not for the sins of the other). I had become increasingly concerned about the trend to rationalize our failings by blaming our family of origin or assigning blame for one's sin or immaturity to abusive people in the past. I frequently saw people using these ideas as an escape, instead of vigorously pursuing a transformed life in Christ.

I didn't want to appear to oppose twelve-step programs or support groups (I don't). Nor did I want to seem impatient with spiritual "turtles," God's slow-grow children. But I did develop a fourteen-point contrast between God's system of healing and the world's system of healing (for example, "Justify or forgive yourself" versus "God has justified and will forgive you" and "Break co-dependence and liberate yourself" versus "Submit to repentance and God's deliverance"). When I gave the message, we distributed a chart summarizing the points.

Such thoroughness is also necessary when discussing awkward subjects. I once did a sermon about masturbation. Although I normally go to the pulpit with only an outline, for that sermon I wrote out nearly a full manuscript. The possibilities for unintentional double-entendres or awkward moments was so great, I spent the extra hours to insure that I had not only the right ideas but the right words. Some sermons require that type of precision.

Although this is hard work for me — and the congregation — I have found that people will listen to a more didactic message patiently and with interest if they care deeply about the subject.

After my Ezekiel message, as I was preparing to dismiss the service, I leaned on the pulpit and said, "I need to tell you, at times like this I feel a real heaviness. I don't apologize for anything I said, but I'm sorry for keeping you so long tonight."

The message was over ninety minutes, and virtually no one moved. After the service and over the following week, I received a flood of comments from people who appreciated my taking the time to do the subject justice.

● *Consider a series.* Sometimes I just can't say all I need to in one sermon. So I occasionally preach a landmark series.

Some especially nettlesome subjects are best approached in stages, that is, with months or years between sermons. I may need to nudge the congregation into the truth, to let them process the Scriptures one step at a time.

That's the way it turned out with my divorce and remarriage sermons. The first sermon addressed the subject of Christians divorced before their conversion; the second sermon, three years later, addressed rare instances when Christians divorced after their conversion may remarry. I didn't calculate this development, but time and understanding helped people digest the teachings.

When appropriate, I branch off into related issues and application. Since so much groundwork has been laid, it's a perfect time to show how this subject relates to other doctrines and practices.

In the message from Ezekiel that addressed the family-of-origin "escape clause," I applied the truths about Christ's power to transform us to how and why we do "altar calls" and "altar services." We have found these times, when we call people to come to the front of the church, to make or renew their commitment or for the laying on of hands, to be one of the most life-transforming steps a Christian can make. I was able to develop the subject more meaningfully than if I had preached "The Purpose of Altar Calls" as a stand-alone message.

● *Relieve the tension.* Landmark sermons address serious, sensitive, sometimes awkward subjects. The tension can be exhausting both for me and the congregation. Relieving that tension two or three times in a long message can make the waters much easier to navigate, and that increases the congregation's ability to receive.

Discrete and timely humor not only breaks the tension but also keeps me human and personable. On the occasion I dealt with a particularly delicate sexual topic, I preceded it with a reading that illustrated the confusion of a camp director: A Victorian prude inquired too obliquely regarding restroom facilities at the camp. The woman's undue caution in not risking suggestive speech set the scene for a hilarious exchange of letters; absence of directness brought no answer whatsoever. It set the atmosphere for me to be direct and also created a sense of "humanness" in the room as we approached a very human subject.

When humor would be inappropriate, I ask people to turn to their neighbor and repeat some positive affirmation. I began the suicide message by announcing to the congregation the title of my sermon and explaining about the death of the individual. I knew everyone was feeling heavy. So I said, "Although we're going to talk about the sin of suicide, I want to remind you that we serve a mighty and merciful God. I'd like for you to turn to the person next to you and gently say, 'We serve a mighty and merciful God.' "

As they said those words, all across the auditorium you could see faces relax somewhat and people shift into more comfortable positions. Everyone was emotionally better able to face what we had to talk about after that.

Sometimes we'll pause for fifteen seconds of praise and thanksgiving for some encouraging truth: "Let's take a moment and praise God for the hope of eternal life with Jesus."

● *Relate personal experience.* Sometimes divulging personal experiences that triggered my message help make the sermon more personal, authentic, and powerful.

When I discussed wine drinking with our leaders, I told them why: I was raised in a teetotaling environment. Years ago, however, I realized how moderate amounts of wine with foods such as pasta or red meat benefited my digestion. I occasionally drank a glass of wine for this reason.

One Saturday morning, about three years after I began this practice, two events changed my habits. First, early in the morning as I was in prayer, the Lord "spoke" clearly to me: I was no longer to drink wine. Nothing I knew of had prompted this "word" to me. It was pointed, and my response was absolutely unhesitant. But, a few hours later the same day, I went to a counseling session not knowing why the wife of a young leader in our congregation had scheduled the appointment. She related how a Christian leader whom we both knew had gone to a restaurant with her husband, drank too much wine, and convinced her husband to think nothing of it. She was understandably troubled.

I didn't say anything to her about how the Lord had dealt with me just hours earlier, but the coincidence of those two events happening on the same morning was not lost on me. I felt God was unmistakably saying, "I'm dealing with you first."

When I recounted this to our leaders, I didn't mandate they act on the basis of my experience; I presented the Scriptures. But my story illustrated the heart of my message and showed how the Lord was teaching about the "cost" of leadership.

● *Symbolize the message when possible.* A few years ago I spoke at an urban conference in Washington D.C. on the subject of reconciliation. About a thousand pastors and leaders attended, 75 percent of whom were black.

In my message I admitted that during the civil-rights movement I had unknowingly, but in reality, violated our unity in Christ. What to the black community was a revival of God's grace in establishing justice, I had viewed as a social inconvenience. Although I agreed that blacks had suffered injustice, when I saw leaders of the Caucasian Christian community marching in demonstrations, I regarded them as liberals straying from the important issues of the gospel. But, too late, I came to realize how many like me had "missed a moment" to appeal in God's name for sacred justice. I said to the group:

"You had a revival that was a great blessing to you, and I

didn't see it. I didn't rejoice with you. I didn't help you. I was not a brother."

At the end of my message I asked one of the black pastors to come forward as a representative. I got down on my knees before him and asked his forgiveness. (I had asked his permission in advance to invite him forward.)

After the service, an aged black elder embraced me and said, "Pastor Hayford, I never thought I'd see the day when a white man would say and do what you did today." The symbolic action riveted the point.

● *Choose the opportune moment.* Since a landmark sermon is a prophetic moment, I can't pencil it on the calendar as I would any other message. Several factors signal when the time is ripe.

Sermons of mine that have proven to be landmarks have been delivered with a strong feeling for God's heart. Often we sacrifice God's love on the altar of his truth. But I have sought to bring both passion for God's holy truth (reflecting his righteous nature) and his endless compassion (which reflects his merciful and loving nature). If either are lacking, the message falls short.

As I prepare a landmark message, I also have a growing sense of anointing best described as a sense of mission and authority. Even before I come into the pulpit, I feel clothed with a mantle of grace to declare a vital word. The message, fully gestated, is ready for birth.

However, events may demand immediate response. When that worship leader in our singles group committed suicide, I felt I had to bring that message within two weeks. World or local events also call for a landmark word on short notice. When responding to the headlines, I must hammer while the iron glows red.

Landmark messages are extraordinarily demanding. They strain my emotions and study time. They force me to wrestle with great issues. They draw criticism. And I know I will have to face some repercussion for people following incorrectly what I say (usually people who didn't listen to all I said).

Despite these pressures, however, as I prepare and deliver

landmark sermons, I commonly have as deep a sense of God's presence as at any time in ministry. As a result, I view landmark sermons as one of the highlights of my pastoral ministry. And shouldering pressure is a small price to pay for a sermon that serves as a can't-miss-it, unshakable oak tree in our church for years to come.

Part 3
Tough Times

Leadership doesn't equal certainty. True leadership sees the inevitable ambiguities of ministry yet has the spiritual sensitivity and resolve to advance through them.

— Ben Patterson

CHAPTER NINE
Do I Always
Have to Be Sure?

When she said, "Now, Pastor, nobody wants you to succeed at this church more than I do," I inwardly groaned. I knew what was coming.

After a year as pastor, I had felt deeply that the church must focus on building leadership for the coming years. So at the previous board meeting I had asked, "I want to find ten men who'll meet with me for a year to study and pray, on the premise that they would go and disciple other men in the church. I want your endorsement for making this my main focus of ministry, with a goal of discipling fifty men over the next five years." They approved what came to be called "Project Mustard Seed."

But now they were having second thoughts. One Sunday morning a board member pulled me aside.

"I think Project Mustard Seed is a great idea," she began, "but maybe if you waited two or three years, the timing would be better. Right now, since you're new, you really need to spend time visiting all the groups in the church and making them feel supported."

I didn't believe that would be a good use of my time. I felt the time for getting to know the congregation had passed; now it was time to develop leaders for the future. But that's when I began to wonder, *How much of Project Mustard Seed is what Ben Patterson wants, and how much really comes from God?*

Even during a family vacation that year to England, the trip of a lifetime, the inner debate never stopped. Two or three times a day, whenever a quiet moment came, that Sunday morning conversation would bubble to the surface. Then I would agonize, again and again, about whether I had made the right choice: *Was it too late to back out? What about the men I'd already asked to participate and who were excited about the program? Suppose the board withdrew its endorsement?*

From that episode I learned that *leadership* doesn't always equal *certainty*. Naturally, we are able to press ahead when we have no doubts. But we live as imperfect people in an imperfect world. True leadership sees the inevitable ambiguities of ministry yet has the spiritual sensitivity and resolve to advance through them.

Here's how I've learned to minister despite uncertainty.

Picking Your Fights

The older I get, I'm more sure of less, and I'm less sure of more! But one thing I've learned is that certitude has a price. The good and wise leader has a clear idea of what issues are worth paying that price (and I suspect it's a fairly short list), and what issues aren't. In my own ministry I've found that, while I may have strong convictions about a subject, it doesn't mean it's always necessary or even advisable to express my certitude in public.

Congregations in America today want it both ways. On the

one hand, people in the pews want the confidence and certainty of a Churchill or Patton, a leader who provides clear answers for their complex lives. But they are also pulled by the cultural impulse that extols individuality, that says "different strokes for different folks."

The church where I grew up required members to sign a thirty-point doctrinal statement. My congregation would consider that an intolerable infringement on their rights. American Christians don't have much stomach for a pastor with a long list of certitudes.

So the issue boils down to two questions: When do I want to be perceived as certain, and when do I want to avoid that perception?

I want to be certain about fundamental doctrines. All but one of Paul's thirteen epistles are written to churches or pastors, and he returns again and again to the theme of preaching a pure gospel: "Then we will no longer be infants, tossed back and forth by the waves, and blown here and there by every wind of teaching and by the cunning and craftiness of men in their deceitful scheming" (Eph. 4:14).

The church in America today is tossed back and forth, so it's vital that we help steady the ship.

Then again, I don't speak *ex cathedra* about programs or policies. The Scriptures contain no doctrine of "pastoral infallibility," no mandate to equate your word with God's. But our stature can tempt us, from time to time, to draw a line in the sand about a particular (and personally heartfelt) program or policy of the church, saying, "This is what God wants, so choose ye this day whom ye shall serve." If any problems arise, however, your credibility suffers. People know better.

I find it helpful to be clear about my expectations. Recently I had an engaged couple in my office for counseling, and as always I asked them, "What are your expectations about the relationship? Things will go smoother after the wedding if you voice your expectations now."

In the same way, I've always approached my church callings as wedding engagements: both parties enter the relationship with expectations, which ought to be expressed up front.

When I was called to my current pastorate, I was candid with the board: "I can't lead this church if you won't let me lead it according to the way I'm put together. If you want Ben Patterson as your pastor, there are certain things that come with the package, things you'll have to live with." I didn't tell them my style of leadership was necessarily right for every church, but it was right for me.

For example, I need time to read and think and pray. I'm not good at tending institutional machinery — I have to delegate that to someone else. I also need the freedom and latitude to take action without tremendous amounts of consensus building. I want to win, and not just keep from losing — even if it means I sometimes shoot from the hip and make mistakes.

"That's what you get with Ben Patterson," I told the board.

I also try to remember the difference between vision and timing. In one church I served, we went through two building programs like clockwork. When a third building project presented itself, my confidence was soaring. We jumped in with both feet, put out brochures, did stewardship meetings, and went whole hog to get the project built in two years.

I was sure about it and talked often and confidently about God's vision for this new building.

But the building didn't get built in two years as predicted. Years later, my successor in that church is just now getting that project together again.

Was my vision wrong? No, but my timing was. Instead of being built in two years, right now it appears the Lord had five to seven years in mind.

Strategies for Straddlers

One season during my high school football days, our coach installed an incredibly high-powered offense — any professional team would have been proud of its complexity. We gave it our best shot, but the complex system was hard for us to learn. Our school was favored to win the opening game, but when the whistle blew our guys ran around the field not sure where they were supposed to go and who they were supposed to block. It's a game we should have won over a smaller high school, but our squad was beaten.

A few days later we sat down to watch a film of the game. On play after play, you could see everyone hesitating on the line of scrimmage. By this time the coach was screaming at us, "If you're going to make a mistake, at least do it aggressively!" Over the years my coach's words have stuck with me. Sometimes in ministry, we're not sure what we're doing, and we hesitate, letting circumstances control us.

Or worse: in some situations pastors have given up altogether. I was visiting one church where only fifty people were scattered across a sanctuary that seated 250. The congregational singing was weak and half-hearted. I wondered why the pastor, who was leading the singing, didn't say, "Let's all get up and move closer together."

Yet as I sat through the service, I started noticing other signs that the pastor had simply given up. The board where the hymn numbers are posted was empty, the sanctuary needed fresh paint, and the sign outside didn't list the times of the services — dozens of little things that said, "I'm too tired for this, and what difference does it make anyway?"

It's easy to get discouraged and give up when you're faced with uncertainty. But it's not all that difficult to adopt strategies of leadership that help project the confidence of a Churchill (a confidence church members want and need), even when on the inside you really feel more like Hamlet.

● *Let us reason together.* Few topics are harder to preach than predestination. Even the apostle Paul had to shrug his shoulders on this subject and say, "Who has known the mind of the Lord?" (Rom. 11:34). So when I preached a sermon last year on predestination, I began by admitting, "I really don't know if anything I'm going to say is true, but this is a doctrine that believers need to deal with, and I'm going to share with you a progress report about my own current thinking on the subject."

Though the hard-core Calvinists were disappointed with me, most of the congregation was glad somebody admitted the subject was open for discussion. "All I can do is give you my best interpretation for now," I told them, "and I make no promise that if I preach again next year I won't have a new point of view. But we need to come to grips with this issue, because making no decision is in itself a decision."

Throughout my sermon the tone of the message was, "Here's what I see, what I feel. Let me tell you why I believe this way, why I'm excited about it, and why I think you should be excited about it, too. Let me try to persuade you, as one Christian to another."

I would never take this approach with fundamental doctrines, but it works with vital doctrines that don't affect salvation. I am forthright about my interpretation, but I give my people the right to disagree with dignity.

At the same time, I'm under no obligation to lay out all the alternatives to my views, being evenhanded with each, suggesting the congregation choose the alternative that best suits them. That's not leadership but an invitation to indecision and paralysis within the church.

I once saw a Christian drama group put on a skit about pastors and their churches called, *That's What We Pay You For*. A committee comes to the pastor telling him that they're upset that in a sermon he gave them two or three possibilities for interpreting a passage. They don't care for that; they're looking for guidance: that's what they pay him for.

A sermon is not a lecture but an occasion where I am called to persuade people to make a deeper commitment to Christ.

● *When the vision gets cloudy.* A friend of mine took a pastorate at a small church in California that shared a building with another congregation. He was convinced the church should build some equity so that someday it could construct a sanctuary of its own. My friend was willing to go fifty-fifty with the congregation in buying a home to serve as a parsonage, with a large enough yard for church picnics and a big family room for small meetings and Bible studies. The church would build equity, the congregation would gain a sense of identity and esteem, and later the house could be sold for the down payment on a new sanctuary.

However, just as the people started getting enthusiastic, my friend began to get cold feet. Did he want to live in a home that wasn't really his? What about the financial and tax complications of going fifty-fifty on the deal? What if he left the church someday? Would the financial entanglement make it harder to leave? Would the church find it harder to recruit a new pastor, since he might not want to be tied to a parsonage?

He had boldly brought forth his idea, and now his credibility as a leader might be at stake if he pulled back. "The people would have thought I was just jerking them around," he later said. "They would have been reluctant to follow my other ideas for fear of being let down again."

My friend adopted a strategy of passivity. He just stopped bringing the parsonage up at the monthly board meetings. If the lay leadership wanted to pursue it, he was prepared to go along. Yet nobody was charged enough to press ahead. Soon the matter died, and my friend wiggled off the hook with his credibility untarnished.

You can't use this strategy often, nor on key decisions that are already in motion (e.g., a building contract has been signed). But once in awhile it gets us out of a jam when uncertainty strikes hard and for good reason.

In general, I try to follow this guideline: I don't back out of a decision because it's becoming unpopular and causing me grief. I feel free to change my mind, though, if people are becoming embittered or losing their faith over the issue. That doesn't settle by itself my uncertainties, but it does help me analyze them better.

● *The realistic cheerleader.* I've always hated cheerleaders who, when the score is 48–0 in favor of the other team, still shout, "Hey, hey, what'dya know, get that ball and go, go, go!" At that point, the players need to hear something like, "We still love you guys!"

Sometimes the church takes a real beating; it looks as if the game is turning into a rout, and as pastors we're not sure whether the team can make a comeback. We're tempted to lead cheers like, "We're looking forward to a great year!" or "God is going to give us the victory!"

What's needed is an honest look at an uncertain situation

combined with confidence about what God can do: "I don't know how it'll turn out, but we are looking to God for guidance" or "This has been hard, but we're going to see God's hand in all this." I call it realistic cheerleading.

● *Writing it down.* It's astounding this power God has given us of being able to put feelings into words, of giving names to things so we can understand them better and gain the victory. That's why I keep a personal journal; it's a place to lay out all the confusions I feel, all the uncertainties, the angers and the fears, to confess them before God in written prayer.

For example, take the night I realized the building project I had been so anxious for was going to grind to an unceremonious halt. When I came home, I began reading the Psalms, and I got to Psalm 132:

> O, Lord, remember David
> and all the hardships he endured.
> He swore an oath to the Lord
> and made a vow to the Mighty One of Jacob:
> "I will not enter my house
> or go to my bed —
> I will allow no sleep to my eyes,
> no slumber to my eyelids
> till I find a place for the Lord,
> a dwelling for the Mighty One of Jacob."

It describes David's struggle to find a place for the Ark. He won't rest until he gets it done.

I wanted to build a sanctuary for God. Our church had studied the theology of worship. We had studied the theology of space. From that we had developed a wonderful theological document. And then we drew up plans that expressed perfectly what we believed about worship. I was so excited about it, but it wasn't going to happen.

After I read about David's struggle, I started writing in my journal — two pages in which I poured out my feelings and questions: "Lord, why did you bring us so far in this thing? Everything seemed so clear up to now; it was going so well. But it has stopped! I've been here fourteen years, and I wanted this to be an exclamation point to my ministry. Now it looks like an asterisk. Lord, help me — help me to continue pursuing this, or help me let go if I need to let go of it."

In taking up pen and paper, the shadows gain shape; I demystify them, give them the human discipline of sentence structure and syntax, and arrive at a way to face the problem.

● *Sometimes he speaks.* We all want to be like Jonah and have God audibly tell us, "Go to Nineveh." No mistake there! Though clear signs don't come as often as we want, I've never been convinced to despair. I am not a Deist, who believes God keeps his distance and lets us solve our own problems. Once in a while, especially when we're attentive, God clarifies our uncertainty.

Earlier I mentioned my doubts about Project Mustard Seed, my program to disciple a small group of men in the church. While I was on vacation in England, I continued to stew over the problem: Should I take the one person's advice to slow down and get to know the congregation better? Or should I reach for the future by training new leaders?

On the final day of our vacation, I toured the annual flower festival in the small Welsh village where we had stayed. As an outreach to the community and a surprise to me, the church that hosted our visit had set up a display with my book, *Waiting,* which had just been published in England. And there by a stack of my books was a flower pot with mustard seeds sprinkled all over the top. I wept because, for me, it was such a powerful confirmation of what I felt God wanted me to do.

● *The certainty of presence.* Walter Wangerin's *The Book of the Dun Cow* is an allegory set in a barnyard with animals as characters (and perhaps the most vivid description of evil I've ever read). In the story, the Holy Spirit is represented as a dun-colored cow that appears at unexpected moments. As characters gaze into her liquid brown eyes and feel her warm breath, her presence nurtures and reassures. Only occasionally does the cow speak, but most of the time she's just there, quietly grazing and observing you with her deep liquid eyes.

I can't conclude this section without stating the obvious,

because it is the obvious I have to keep reminding myself of: there are no guarantees in life. My family, my health, my church can be devastated in a moment. But one thing is certain: God is present. And the most reliable strategy for facing the uncertainties of ministry is to trust in the God who is always there, quietly gazing at us with deep liquid eyes. As Psalm 73 puts it:

When my heart was grieved
    and my spirit embittered,
I was senseless and ignorant;
    I was a brute beast before you.
Yet I am always with you;
    You hold me by my right hand.
You guide me with your counsel,
    and afterward you will take me into glory.
Whom have I in heaven but you?
    And earth has nothing I desire besides you.

Over the Falls

In discussing the issue of vocation at life's different stages, Karl Barth notes that younger pastors are usually the ones who boldly plunge ahead, while older men often play things close to the vest — they've been through the mill before, or perhaps they have more to lose.

Then Barth asks the rhetorical question, "Does the river slow down as it approaches the falls?"

The answer, of course, is that the river gains speed, rushing fastest at the very moment it plunges over the edge. I want my ministry to pick up speed as I go along. I don't want to be careless and wantonly make mistakes; I want to use the wisdom God has given me to follow the bends that life presents. But as I face uncertainty, I don't want to trickle off into some side stream. I want to be like that river, rushing toward the falls — and when I go over the edge, I look forward to falling into the arms of God.

How our stand is received is determined more by how we treat people than how we marshal our argument.
— *Jack Hayford*

CHAPTER TEN

Taking the Unpopular Stand

At a convention attended by several thousand ministers and church leaders, I was scheduled to bring the second plenary message. The first speaker was a close friend, and as I sat on the platform listening to his message, I was deeply troubled.

He was speaking about a prominent leader who had recently failed morally. Yet in his effort to show forgiveness and acceptance, I felt he was glossing over the biblical requirements for being restored to leadership. I was more troubled when the majority of the congregation responded with applause and amens. They were affirming the principle of forgiveness, which I, of course, fully endorsed. But they were not being led to discern the other side of the issue: this leader must, by biblical standards, enter a time of accountable restoration.

I was about to follow my friend in the pulpit, and my spirit was pressed to bring balance into the situation. But how could I do that without embarrassing and alienating a dear and respected friend? Without spilling ice water on the conference? Without sounding like a Pharisee?

I was at a loss. I was traveling with a pastoral staff member, who was seated beside me on the platform, and I leaned over and admitted, "I don't know if I can get up and speak."

An unpopular stand is never easy but sometimes necessary: to confront unbalanced teachings, tether straying programs, address financially wasteful practices, or lead where no one has thought of going or was willing to lead before.

Unlike the best-selling book title, influencing people doesn't always win friends. Like Caleb and Joshua, who were nearly stoned when they insisted on going into the Promised Land, our unpopular stand can lead to the loss of consensus or momentum, alienate leaders, or even get us fired or excommunicated.

But that doesn't have to be the case. Having taken a number of unpopular stands over the years, I've learned a few things that have prevented Hayford's Last Stand.

Danger from Within

An unpopular stand is dangerous not only from without but especially from within. We risk sins of the heart. We may be sorely tempted in a number of ways.

No matter how many verses buttress my belief, how much my experience bolsters my position, or how many people support my cause, if I assume I cannot and have not missed something on an issue, then I've surrendered to pride. All of us do have some truth, but none of us has all the truth. We can know "truths," including knowing Christ, the Truth. But that doesn't mean that any of us should presume that we know it all.

For example, if there's anything I'm convinced of, it is of my own sinfulness and need of the Savior. But no matter how fully I have grieved over past sin or how despicable present temptation may be to me, I'm a fool if I suppose I understand all the depth of all the evil inherent in "sin." Surely I know evil is wrong, but who among us grasps the full dimensions of evil?

If so foundational a truth as sin's sinfulness outstrips my full comprehension, how much more the controversial and less developed themes of Scripture!

I also have to be careful not to overreact. One year because I was speaking out of town several days prior to our Palm Sunday program, I missed the final rehearsal. Our music director gave me a tape of the rehearsal, to help prepare me to emcee the program.

As I listened to the cassette, one number, a rendition of "The Old Rugged Cross" orchestrated and arranged by some of our musicians, troubled me. The song seemed too jazzy. Our church employs most musical styles, so jazz was not of itself a problem. But following an earlier seasonal program, we had agreed with our musicians to employ only one jazz arrangement per program. By my count "The Old Rugged Cross" was the second jazz piece in the Easter program.

What irked me, however, was that halfway through the song our saxophone improvisation "tore it up." Even at the rehearsal the choir had begun cheering, captivated by the performance and oblivious to the song's theme. I thought, *They're cheering the death of Jesus Christ! They're not cherishing the old rugged cross. They're cheering a guy having a fit on a horn!* I was furious.

Since the program was to take place that night, I immediately called Jim, our music director, and asked him to come to my office. When we met, I was angry.

When my fury was spent, Jim said, "Jack, the last thing I want is to do something that would hurt you this much."

"I don't know what to do," I said, a little more controlled now. "I can't handle this number. Of course, I understand your problem: everyone's worked hard on it, and we can't just say, in effect, 'We don't like you, and we don't like your song.' "

Jim ventured further, patient with my frustration: "Jack, do you know how the arrangement came about?"

I didn't know, obviously, so Jim suggested I meet with Bob, the arranger of the song, to get his perspective.

Just two hours before the program, we met in my office. I learned that in the musicians' minds, the song wasn't technically a jazz number, so, to begin, he hadn't violated our "one-jazz-arrangement" policy. He went on to explain that the saxophone's intent in the improvisation was to express his exhilaration over being set free by Christ's death on the cross, that at "The Old Rugged Cross" his sins were taken away! As I interacted further I was moved to tears. I knew what I would do.

That night at the concert, before "The Old Rugged Cross," I took time to "set up" the song. I said frankly, "Some of you might misunderstand the upcoming song. The arrangement could offend you. But let me invite you to hear a story first." I called Bob to the microphone, and he explained his feelings, which included a beautiful testimony of how he first conceived the arrangement.

During the song, God's presence was powerfully felt. I didn't invite people to make a decision to follow Christ at that moment (though we did later), but I could have. Like my wife, many who usually do not appreciate jazz told me afterward they loved it.

Instead of a disaster, with musicians in revolt or half the congregation offended, "The Old Rugged Cross" became a highlight of the evening. That would have been lost, however, if Jim, our music director, had not graciously weathered my blast and helped me wisely tackle a difficult situation. Temper tantrums, extremism, and knee-jerk decisions can cut the legs from beneath a leader taking an unpopular stand.

I also try to avoid the temptations to debate or prematurely attack. Because we are tempted to assume that "God waves my flag," we "cavalry charge" into an unpopular stand, seeking to out-argue our "opponents." But crossing swords is hardly the best way to enlist supporters.

Trying to help everyone understand each other better accomplishes more. Usually we labor against stereotypes of the opposition. Dialogue helps us deal honestly with what people really think.

Furthermore, if the broader body of Christ is struggling with an issue, we may be wiser to wait before hastening comment. I don't have to verify my prophetic role by being the first to address a tough subject. Christian journals are often the best forum for looking at controversial topics. In fact, we'll sometimes distribute articles in the congregation for their consideration.

Instead of saying, "This is what I believe about school prayer," I'm wiser sometimes to say, " Have you heard Jim Dobson's recent and helpful comments?" In other words, as a pastor I don't always have to mount a horse and be the first to charge into battle.

Motives that Motivate

The purer our motives, the higher the ground we stand on — and the more likely people will give us a hearing. Here are five motives I want to have.

● *To promote unity.* In 1989, the Lausanne Congress on World Evangelism invited me to speak at their Manila conference on the subject, "Signs and Wonders in Evangelism." I was specifically asked also to lead in an extended time of worship and prayer following my message.

My objective was not to argue a viewpoint. Rather, I had been asked to deal with this theme because honest leaders, of all doctrinal and denominational stripes, acknowledged that God is doing mighty miracles all over the world. The implications for all our evangelistic ministries are great, so the conference leadership wanted the subject addressed. I was humbled to be asked, of course, and I sought to be gracious and thorough in presentation.

Afterward as I walked back to my hotel, it was dark, and a line of people behind and before me moved slowly. Among the conversations, I heard someone ahead say, referring to my message, "Praise God! There's one for our side."

When I heard that, I ached. I hadn't unleashed a broadside, and I had no desire to break people into camps. I had intended to promote unity by calling attention to a larger truth (and many people affirmed I did). But this one person seemed to think only in terms of a "fight," and unity as a goal was hardly understood.

● *To avoid polemics.* When and if I take an unpopular stand, I do so not merely because I believe it's true but also because I believe it's life. Jesus called himself the way, the truth, and the life, and watching him we see how he presented truth: fostering and nourishing life. A good surgeon doesn't slash, gouge, and rip out but cuts delicately and gently — to heal.

Ultimately people are more important to God than principles. I don't mean that I sacrifice principles, because right principles always further our welfare. But if we only relate to principles, as simply truth and not as truth to set people free, we'll end up arguing for mere principles, violating the heart of God.

For example, I'm a strong believer in tithing, which for some is an unpopular stand. Recently, some months after I had spoken on tithing, a staff member informed me that one couple was downgrading their affiliation with our church from membership to partnership status (the membership commitment includes a commitment to tithe). And they were not the only ones in the church for whom tithing was suddenly becoming controversial. I also learned that two prominent radio ministers had recently argued against tithing in a series of messages; they felt it wasn't a New Testament idea.

In response I wrote an article for our church publication. I didn't wage an assault on the radio speakers or the people in our church, but I did confront the issue. I approached it from the perspective of God's goodness — wanting to bring, through "release" of our tithing, a beautiful financial and spiritual release. The purpose of tithing, I communicated, is life not law.

I later went to the home of a couple who were unsure about tithing and felt hurt by my article. I didn't argue with them. I simply loved them. I emphasized that God wasn't against them, nor was I. I wasn't there to stomp out heresy but to help people find life in God's Word and ways.

● *To bring discernment.* Real life problems are complex, often too complex to be answered with one or two proof texts. Only through mature discernment can we understand God's heart, understand Scripture in context, and see how Scripture applies to individual situations. Rather than tossing a blanket principle over every problem, I seek to foster understanding. Well-discerned truth fosters life and never violates truth or love.

● *To build, maintain, or strengthen relationships.* If I "set people straight" but alienate or offend them, what have I gained? I may be right, but my approach has been wrong. In the end I probably do more harm than good; I will not have served any value beyond my own self- or cause-justifying efforts.

So in the process of taking an unpopular stand, I hope to make friends, not enemies. Even though there will be disagreement, I want to build a relationship so we can communicate in the future. If I bruise or break off relations, my input into a person's life is over, so I need to "speak the truth in love."

Many times after I have taken an unpopular stand or presented an opposing position, people have said to me, "I still don't agree with what you said, but I never heard anybody say it like that." They've not become my enemy. I may not have won them to my position, but I have won them relationally.

People Skills

Whether or not our stand is well-received is determined more by how we treat people than how we marshal our argument. The spirit in which I take my stand is as important as what I say. Six guidelines enable me to champion a cause in a generous, gracious, and loving fashion.

1. Acknowledge how my stand affects others. I try not to take a stand until I feel empathy and compassion — until I understand what my stand will mean to the other party, how it is difficult or painful for them. For example again, when I challenge people to tithe, I may say, "Tithing may seem impossible for you. You may feel I'm asking you to live in religious poverty or ignore your financial obligations. Worse, you might suspect I'm trying to build a church program at your expense.

"Nothing could be farther from the truth. I know you have to pay utilities and a mortgage, buy shoes for your kids and eventually send them to college. I want you to have everything you need and more. I want to see your home and finances blessed by God in a way you could never accomplish yourself. And I believe God ordains that when we tithe."

2. *Respect the motives of dissenters.* I respect others when I recognize (a) they are as committed to truth as I am, and (b) they believe they are serving some worthy value or ideal.

To some extent, all of us have mixed or undiscerned motives, but few of us intentionally and maliciously seek wrong. Granted, some who oppose our stand may be uninformed or misguided, but we need to remember they might not realize that. I need to relate to what they think they're doing.

So I try to discover what values others are serving. What are their goals? What is most important to them? What is at stake for them and why?

When I became angry with our musicians over the Easter program, I listened to their case. Having a respect for their intent, I said, "We all want the same thing: We want to minister to people. We want to serve this church. We want to worship Christ. Please help me see how this song does that."

By respecting that my perceived opponent has a right motive, a climate of love and understanding can be fostered. Especially as it concerns church direction, we can work together. I can help promote their goals or help them see how my goals serve their values. We can discuss options that help us both fulfill the values we think are important.

If I don't give options that serve others' values, I force people to buy into my position. I'd rather try to find a win-win solution.

3. *Acknowledge the truth in dissenters' positions.* Especially if I'm about to oppose a popular view, I have to assume that the popular position has some inherent truth. Undoubtedly, verses can be marshaled as "proof texts."

Therefore I genuinely concede any truth in others' positions. I do so with conviction, not as a patronizing concession, not like a baseball pitcher who uses a slow, benign windup only to uncork a 100 MPH, high, inside fastball, bent on intimidating the batter.

For example, most in my denomination want to hold a dispensational approach to the Book of Revelation. I knew when I departed from that position, some might equate that change with something tantamount to denying the Virgin Birth. But by affirming the scholarship that lay behind the prevailing view, I allayed doubts and gained a hearing.

After I acknowledge the truth in someone else's position, of course, like Paul Harvey I give the rest of the story.

4. Approach issues positively. In the conference mentioned in the introduction of this chapter, I did find the wherewithal to step to the pulpit and preach. Rather than clubbing my friend, however, I began from a positive stance, describing our calling to a priestly ministry of praise, and as priests, to a life of holiness and purity before the Lord. I spoke about how the priests had to exemplify holiness to the congregation, how they had to meet certain requirements as leaders, and then applied that to the leaders who had fallen.

People respond more favorably to a positive approach. The positive approach points people in a specific, attractive direction. Feistiness is the product of self-righteousness. But humility breeds a positive approach. It will leave people wanting to do the right thing, and for the right reason. They understand more fully why the right is right, rather than just why the wrong is wrong. A positive approach shows others you are interested in them — not just in being right. It is virtually impossible to criticize most people without being perceived as attacking them.

5. Affirm your relationship. "These men who have fallen are my friends," I assured those attending the convention. "Despite any failures, I respect them. I don't want to say or do anything that would hinder that friendship."

Opponents of my stand need to know I identify with them. We are on the same side, in the same camp, on the same team. Although we now differ over an issue, that issue will not rupture our relationship. No matter what position they take, I'm committed to them; I'm for them. I demonstrate that acceptance by going out of my way to greet them warmly and acknowledge them.

6. *Attend to the heart.* One of the most unfruitful assumptions we can make is that we can change, reach, or grow people primarily through their brain. When you take an unpopular stand, information, facts, and logic may seem to you to prove your point, but they will seldom win your detractors. So I try to reach others through their hearts, through love and respect for them, through showing them how my emotions have been affected by the issue, through telling them I deeply care about the issue and them.

This characterizes my efforts and approach whether I'm dealing with a fellow Christian (say, of a different doctrinal stance) or a fellow citizen of my nation (say, who supports gay rights). In each case, though we may disagree significantly we share something in common, even if it's only our humanity.

One pastor I know felt the need to change his church's name. The current name described his church in theological terms, which confused those unfamiliar with his denomination. But he also knew a name change could seem to be a slap in the face to his leaders, and he knew that logic alone wouldn't win them over.

So he proposed the idea to some of the leaders in an exploratory fashion, acknowledging, "I know our church's name is important to you, and I value your feelings and respect our tradition. I don't want to appear to walk over anyone's feelings. But could you help me? I think possibly a new name could help us be more accessible, help us more effectively reach out to the unchurched."

Acknowledging the feelings of the older leaders helped his elders respond flexibly. A key leader in the church said, "You're right. If we change the name, it will be like losing an old friend. But let's think of a way to affirm our history yet be open to tomorrow. If a new name will help others find the Lord, I certainly want to be open."

They did. And within a short time, their church did change the name without conflict.

The Right Time to Take a Stand

The timing of our stand influences how it will be received. Here are some indicators of the right moment.

For instance, I try to take a stand when it will least embarrass others. I probably could have avoided that stressful confrontation with my friend's ideas on the convention platform. The night before at a banquet for forty leaders, my friend had made similar comments. His words troubled me then, but I didn't say anything, even in private. Of course, I didn't know he would repeat his words the next day before the huge conference crowd. If I had guessed he might do as much, I would have gone to him and raised questions personally. I believe he would have at least balanced his comments the next day and probably omitted them completely.

I'll also take a stand when it's now or never. Although on that Palm Sunday afternoon, after four morning services, I was not in the best mood to talk to the musicians, there was no time to lose. Under such circumstances, I don't wait until I have all the answers before I begin talking to people. I need information and perspective before I ensconce myself in a position that can become unpopular. I admit, "I don't know what to do right now, but I know we need to talk."

But such urgency is the exception: in the local church few things have to be said right now. There are usually other meetings coming up or another means of communication that will make understanding easier, and so reduce the likelihood of conflict.

Of course, I want to wait until God gives clear direction. For example, we were bogged down over an issue at our denominational business meeting. As I reread the resolution in question, I noticed that by changing one word the controversy could be solved. I went to the microphone, acknowledged the validity of both arguments, and then proposed the word change that would please both sides.

It was accepted, and the resolution passed promptly. As I reflected later, I concluded that God had spoken that single word into my heart. There is no better time to act than when we feel God has given "a word of wisdom."

Dealing with the Fallout

To take an unpopular stand always holds the possibility of

unpleasant fallout. I don't count on it — I hope to avert it. I relate to people gently so as to prevent it. But there are no limits to how people can misread one another. Then I have to patch up relationships. I may have to explain and re-explain. I need to keep my ear to the ground to learn if others may misinterpret me.

For example, if I know someone quits a church duty or leaves the church, I try to do one of two things, if there is any chance that will help. First, I accept the responsibility for the "failure" they perceive has taken place. I figure there is no use arguing my righteousness. By their views, we've done or said something that should not have been done or said. I don't apologize for what's been done (unless an apology is in order); I simply acknowledge my role in the affair and my concern about their leaving.

Second, if I can do it in good conscience, if it's a matter of Christian disagreeing with Christian, I'll "bless them," literally announcing my favor about their decision, so they leave without any rancor against me or me against them.

The result is that most people feel "heard" and "understood," and many return to their responsibility or to membership.

During any unpopular stand, my goal is less to win friends than to influence people. But I've found that by speaking the truth with a spirit of love, respect, and consideration, friendship and influence often go hand in hand.

Personal and leadership frustrations are intertwined. The pressure comes from several directions: our insecurities, our children, our spouse, the church board. But who we are as a person ties it all together.
— Leith Anderson

CHAPTER ELEVEN
When You're Tired of Leading

P reaching that Sunday was the last thing I wanted to do.

The church where I'd been serving as a part-time associate had indicated they would put me on staff full time. A few days after my seminary graduation, however, I was terminated. The congregation held a business meeting and voted me out.

I was devastated. Charleen, my wife, and I were so anticipating seminary's end and full-time ministry. We also needed the income. Without a job, the short-term financial picture looked bleak.

The senior pastor went on vacation, and I was scheduled to speak the following Sunday, four days after receiving my pink slip. Since it was too late in the week to recruit a pinch hitter, the congregation asked me to fill in for the vacationing minister.

So I did, despite the awkwardness of the situation. I recognized I couldn't walk into the pulpit that Sunday morning spewing frustration at the congregation. Nor could I, in good conscience, refuse to speak. I felt that preaching God's Word in that situation was the right thing to do.

This was a painful lesson in doing the right thing, despite my mood at the time. Pastors, at least in that sense, are professionals. God's people have a right to competent leadership, even when we're feeling tired, angry, frustrated, or lonely. Knowing this doesn't make leading easy at such times, but it's the first principle, of many, that has helped me lead when I haven't felt like it.

Shirt-Sleeve Symptoms

How I happen to feel at any given moment is not a good indication of fatigue level. Sometimes I'm running on adrenalin and feel great, but I'm "high" only because my weary body has had to kick in extra juice to keep going.

So I've found it helpful over the years to monitor my feelings and behavior. For example, I know I'm fatigued when my emotions are out of control. Feelings are harder to control than intellect. Even when rational decisions are made, our emotions can lag far behind.

Too many times I have allowed an isolated comment by one individual to balloon in my mind until my emotions are raw. There is a temptation to fantasize a single criticism into a congregational mutiny. Thoughts race wildly from defense to offense to surrender or retreat.

When these feelings are way out of proportion to the reality of the situation, it's probably because I'm worn out from many other things. Like the straw that broke the camel's back, the last item is what upset me, but there's a lot more behind it.

Chronic tiredness, headaches, sleeping too much, or insomnia are also flashing yellow lights of frustration and tiredness.

After my first two years of ministry (I was 26 years old) everything was getting me down. Outwardly most of ministry was going great; inwardly I couldn't shake off constant discouragement that bordered on depression. I was tired all the time. Motivation lagged. I knew something was wrong, but I didn't know what.

I never thought about going to a doctor about my problems, but I did make an appointment because of a sore throat and swollen glands. His diagnosis was swift and certain: mononucleosis. I talked him out of hospitalizing me on the promise I would get lots of rest.

What I thought was a spiritual or emotional or psychological problem was actually a physical illness. Once rested and recuperated, the earlier problems disappeared.

Having trouble focusing on a task is a less obvious fatigue symptom. Sometimes when I'm preparing a sermon and concentration wanders to all the things I have yet to do, I can trace it back to a subtle emotional fissure.

When I'm tired, angry, or resigned, I may deal with people in ways that dig a deeper hole for myself. I might make a comment in a board meeting or in another setting that sets someone off. Then I find myself in a loop of offending and apologizing.

Another sign of leadership fatigue: looking through the classifieds. In early years of ministry, I'd sometimes flip through the classified section of the Sunday *Denver Post* and think, *What else could I do for a living?* I discovered that having a master of divinity degree wasn't much use for anything else. The one job that intrigued me was driving eighteen wheelers.

What I see now is that looking through the classifieds wasn't a harmless diversion. I did that because I was frustrated with ministry and weary of trying to make it work.

Fatigue Factors

What saps a leader's optimism and boundless energy isn't always readily apparent. Often I can't point to a criticism or a long week as the source of my infection. Sometimes its beginning is imperceptible.

I've also discovered that what I was susceptible to ten years ago may not affect me today. Here is a collage of contributing factors draining the energy reservoir throughout my years in ministry.

● *Learning the ropes.* Entry level pastoral experience is tiring. We've gone to school but don't know how to handle pastoral situations.

Early in my ministry, a younger woman in the church with grade school children was diagnosed with a brain tumor. The last weeks of her life were painful as her life slowly ebbed away.

Being inexperienced, I didn't know what to do. Nor did I know the deceased or her family well. So at her funeral, I did what I had seen others do: I read her obituary from the local newspaper and attempted to make the funeral as personable as possible. Then I preached a brief message.

After an awkward silence, because I didn't know how to end a funeral, the widower (he had recently been in an automobile accident) stood up, clutched his crutches, and staggered to where I was standing. I waited. Upon reaching me, he bent over and whispered loudly, "You forgot my son."

In reading the family survivors, I had missed a son whom I didn't know existed. His name wasn't mentioned in the obituary.

I was devastated. *I've just poured myself into this funeral,* I thought, *and all her husband will remember is that I forgot to mention his son.* I drove home, emotionally tapped out.

Every new experience — the first time dealing with the deacon board, the first Easter, the first Christmas, the first child death, the first wedding — wore me down.

● *Ineffective leadership.* Many leaders get bogged down by creating too many close relationships in their congregation. Their leadership is like the hub-and-spoke wheel: the pastor is the hub, and the spokes are relationships in the church.

What tires a pastor is servicing all these relationships. Mrs. Black is upset because the pastor doesn't visit her, so the pastor visits her. Mr. Thompson is angry because the pastor doesn't call on his parents, so the pastor fits them into a busy schedule. The relationships are based on the pastor's ability to meet everyone's needs.

In a smaller church, of two hundred or less, that might work. But as a church grows, the pastor must carefully choose ministry relationships, moving to a more hierarchical model: the pastor relates to a few individuals who then each relate to a few more, until the whole congregation is ministered to.

Fewer, stronger relationships will not only enable the church to grow but also keep your emotional well-being intact.

● *Criticism.* In the late sixties and early seventies, my family and I lived in a church parsonage. During those years, housing prices were skyrocketing, and so I concluded we needed to buy a house before inflation put housing out of financial reach. I approached the church trustees, asking if they would sell the parsonage and provide an adequate salary adjustment, enabling us to purchase a home.

They agreed and recommended the proposal at the next congregational meeting. A few dissented, but the motion passed. Excited, Charleen and I then picked out a lot and had blueprints drawn up. Several contractors in our church — electrical, plumbing, painting — offered their services at cost. We would be able to build a $30,000 dollar house for $20,000. We were ecstatic.

But then some snipers took aim. "You're just using the church for your own purposes," we heard. "You're in the ministry for the money." Other cutting remarks followed. The personal attacks, though from a vocal minority, became so hard to handle that my wife and I called off the project.

I was hurt. I eventually resolved my emotions about that issue, but hearing personal criticism still tires me.

● *Always being the answer man.* I've never felt compelled to be in charge of every situation. Just because I'm a pastor, I don't have to coach the church softball team or take charge of every meeting. Uncomfortable silence may fall over the dinner table when eating in a restaurant. Many people defer to me even in a nonchurch setting. *He's the pastor,* they think. *He should pray.* I've chuckled inwardly as people wait for me to bless the food. Sometimes I do; other times I reach for my fork.

But at church, the buck does stop with me; I am the leader. And I can tire of that. Some days, walking thirty feet of hallway, from the reception area to my office, takes thirty minutes as I have to stop and answer questions and give input to staff and others.

As pastor I'm also often asked to make hard decisions about funerals or baptisms or weddings or building use.

About a year ago, we rented our facility to an outside organization. The church board decided on a rental fee, but it was never collected. A couple of weeks ago, someone from that organization called saying, "I think we owe you $1,000, but we're not going to be able to pay." Wooddale had no record of an accounts receivable from them.

So, a decision had to be made about our records. Then the accountant had to be contacted. And on it went. When many such decisions are mixed with physical weariness, I can feel overwhelmed.

● *Incompleteness.* A frequent source of our struggles in ministry is the lack of closure. Our tasks never appear finished.

A friend of mine pastored a church in the Chicago area. He remodeled his house, adding a new bathroom. After a day at the church, he would head for home, go into the new bathroom, even before speaking to his wife, and flush the toilet. He needed to know something that he did was completely finished. When the toilet flushed, he knew for sure he was finished with the bathroom. His job was complete. And it worked!

Ministry is more like soccer than baseball. Baseball is played with more order: the game proceeds, pitch by pitch, you try to touch four bases (and always in the same order), and everyone clearly has a position on the field. Soccer is more fluid: there are no long pauses in play, you run in all sorts of directions, at moments it's hard to see who is playing what position.

In the church, people don't always run in the same direction nor do they stay in their positions! Furthermore, it's difficult to figure out when you've succeeded or failed in the pastorate. When is your sermon finally honed enough for Sunday? When is everyone needing care attended to? When is Sunday's attendance high enough? When is there enough money to go around? Living in such fluidity, with questions that can never be fully answered, can be tiring.

● *Internal pressure to succeed.* I have a nephew who pastors a church in the shadow of Willow Creek Church, where over 16,000 worshipers from the Chicago area attend weekly. Though growing and ministering effectively to its community, his "David" church is relatively small in comparison to the "Goliath" a few miles away. But my nephew appreciates the effective ministry of Willow Creek and doesn't chafe because his church isn't the same.

Comparing ourselves to others' Olympic standards can be frustrating. Our internal motivations to succeed, based on others' success, can make us driven and perpetually dissatisfied. Our interpretation of success and failure is often the mother lode of leadership fatigue.

● *Breaking the "rules."* When policies or guidelines are regularly broken, it not only hampers the ministry of the church, it tires me out. I get frustrated with people, and I have to take extra time and effort to put things back into line.

Wooddale Church has a policy book covering building use, the hiring process, staff procedures, salary guidelines, bus use, and much more. I became frustrated when I learned that some staff members followed policies while others did not. They weren't deliberately breaking the rules; they forgot what the policies were.

So I invited the pastoral staff to our home for a one-day retreat. I read and explained the history and rationale for every policy — it took about six hours. That day has become a legend.

True, what I did was triggered by frustration, but it worked! Now I hear staff members tell each other to know and follow policies or "we'll end up spending a whole day with Leith reading the policy book again."

Which Is It: Me or My Job?

I find that my physical state can exacerbate my feelings about leadership, so I make a distinction between being tired of leading and just plain being tired.

I've been up Saturday night with a sick child and still had to preach the next morning. By Sunday evening, I'm exhausted. And then I become vulnerable to being discouraged by whatever happens to be the crisis of the day. I'm weighed down with my sick child or my physical or mental health. When this happens, my emotions usually turn around in a day or so.

Being tired of leadership, though, is a deeper tiredness. When the church I pastored in Colorado voted down a proposal to hire a part-time associate pastor, someone I felt the church needed, something inside of me changed. Though the church's leadership was on board with the plan, my proposal died on the floor of a church business meeting.

Sitting in the meeting that evening, I thought, *If every decision is going to be based on finances and if people are going to block continually this church's mission, I can't invest the rest of my life here.*

I had been frustrated before, but usually I felt better within 48 hours. This time I began thinking, *How much energy can I keep pouring into something that is not going to get an adequate return, especially considering my gifts and goals?* The feeling didn't go away for months. I knew I had leadership fatigue.

Personal and leadership issues, in the final analysis, are intertwined. Our frustration comes from different directions: our insecurities, our children, our spouse, the church board. But who we are as a person ties it all together.

Rx for Fatigue

Through the years, I've discovered I have the ability to take a bad situation and make it worse. So when I'm feeling down, besides eating right and getting enough sleep and exercise, I've taken precautions to lessen or resolve ministry frustrations.

● *Be selective with whom you confide.* I want to be frank with the congregation about my weaknesses and struggles — up to a point. But I don't have the right to dump my personal problems on the people.

An open display of rampant emotion might invoke initial sympathy, but questions about competence and spirituality will inevitably arise. In doing so, we destabilize the situation even more.

When a leader shares his personal problems in a broad context, people feel helpless.

When I'm down, I'm careful with whom I confess my struggles. The fewer who know of my condition the better — though it is critical that I talk with someone.

The first person I talk to is my wife. Charleen has had greater positive spiritual impact on my life than anyone. She was God's agent in my life at age 15 when we started dating and still is today.

I talk to others, including fellow pastors on the staff, elders, trusted friends in the church, and lifelong colleagues who make up a network of friends across America.

● *Stay with the ship.* An extended leave of absence, though the most desirable option when you feel burned out, is often ministry suicide. You so remove yourself from the situation that while you're gone, the dynamics change. Just like marriage, the trial separation becomes a harbinger of divorce. Leaves of absence often lead to departures within twelve to twenty-four months.

Instead, I urge burned-out leaders to deal with their issues in short-term departures — two to three weeks — or remain in the saddle, cutting back hours and responsibility.

One pastor friend took a year-long sabbatical. When he returned to the church, he warmly explained, "I've changed!" He liked the way he had changed. They liked him better as he was before, however, and fired him.

Then there's the untidy matter of the Lord's call to another ministry. Knowing whether the time has come to move on is complex — especially when I feel under the gun. So when I'm tired and thinking of leaving, I write down in detail what's happening: my emotions, conversations, events. Then I tuck this "diary" in an envelope and shove it in a desk drawer, deciding not to pull it out for six months or a year.

This exercise does two things. First, it gives me emotional release. Because of an impending date I've set, I know I won't have to endure this frustration forever. The end is in six months or a year. And if after six months of prayer and consideration I still feel like moving on, I'm more likely to do so. Most of the time, though, I discover that I can hardly remember the intensity of the emotions I felt six months earlier.

Second, it gives me a place to vent emotions. Journaling is widely known for its therapeutic value. Writing leaves a permanent record, which allows me to reread what I wrote. Having the process on paper (or disk) shows how much emotions and circumstances do change with time.

● *Monitor the critical areas.* Al Sloan, the board chairman who led General Motors to a significant spurt in growth, said that he made decisions in two critical areas: personnel and money. Monitoring just those two areas gave him sufficient control to help the company succeed.

Leading a church, I've often mused, may be more complicated than running General Motors. But at a minimum — even in frustrating and volatile times — pastors need to stay abreast of key personnel decisions, finances, and preaching. Even when we're angry, moody, lonely, and discouraged, the stakes are too high to ignore these vital areas.

I've lost track of how many pastors have told me they desperately needed to hire an assistant immediately but didn't have time to search for candidates or research references. So they hired the easiest and most available person. Twelve months later there was conflict, disappointment, and sometimes termination. You can't be too busy to recruit the right staff.

● *Communicate frustrations.* I need to talk through my frustrations. I need to describe what I'm feeling and hear the other person's perspective. That prevents bitterness and anger from festering and keeps fatigue to a minimum.

I've been blessed by outstanding elder-board chairmen at Wooddale Church. Each one has responded to one or more calls to hear me vent frustration about some person, a building construction problem, staff decision, or personal problem. They hear me out. They make suggestions. They calm me down. Without exception they have de-escalated my rising emotions.

● *Be self-aware.* When I pastored in Colorado, Charleen and I attended Saturday night church socials and parties. However, I tired of getting home late only to have to get up early and preach the next morning. But after being at church parties for ten years, we couldn't say, "We're not going to do this anymore." The expectations were set in cement.

So when our family arrived at Wooddale, we decided to protect our Saturday evenings. Not long after, there was an usher's dinner on a Saturday night.

"I'll buy your ticket, Pastor," said an enthused church leader. "My wife and I would like your family to sit at our table."

"We'd loved to sit with you, but we won't be at the dinner," I replied. "We don't go out on Saturday nights." He was surprised and disappointed, but I knew better than to agree to go.

Strength Through Weakness

Ministry fatigue is to be avoided. It usually makes everything worse — self, church, family, and friendships — when we wear ourselves down.

But I couldn't close this chapter without mentioning a paradox: often when I've been at my lowest, I've found God to be at his best. My weariness is reinforced with his pylons of strength. And that has been a wonderful experience. The times I didn't want to preach but stepped into the pulpit anyway, I've heard, "God really touched my life through that sermon." Christ was lifted up.

For instance, God also honored my decision to preach the Sunday after my seminary graduation.

"Why don't you stay on staff until you find another job," the church countered after that unforgettable Sunday. Later that summer the senior pastor resigned, and the church voted overwhelmingly to make me their senior pastor.

It's easy but inappropriate for ministry to revolve around me — my needs, my gifts, my ability to get things done. That's a setup for a sinful ego trip. Christ is exalted in my weakness, inadequacy, and desperation. Weariness can become the greatest opportunity for leadership — because then I must lean on God and his provision of grace.

The upside of loneliness is that it puts me in touch with my own needs — my need of God, my need of love, my need of other people.

— Ben Patterson

CHAPTER TWELVE

Must Leaders Be Lonely?

We were gathered in my living room, and the committee meeting had just started when Cliff, one of our board members, took me aside and asked if we could talk privately. We went into my study. My desk lamp was the only light in the room, so a shadowy gloom surrounded us. As it turned out, the gloom was entirely appropriate to what Cliff had to say.

"I don't believe in mincing words," he began stiffly, "so I'll just come out with it. I'm resigning from the board, and I'm taking my family out of the church."

"Why?" I asked, stunned.

"You and I haven't agreed on much since this church began," Cliff continued. "We just keep stepping on each other's toes. I need to be where I can support the pastor and the direction of the church. And you need to have people on your team who back your leadership. This is for your good as well as mine."

That hurt. Cliff was the third layperson in the previous two weeks to resign from leadership. The first had given me the sandpaper side of his tongue on the way out. The second had been gracious. Cliff's style was all business, blunt and to the point. Despite the differences in their styles, all three gave the same reason for resigning: me.

It was my first pastorate, and it was a new church development to boot. We didn't even have a church building yet. I was green, I was scared, and I was exhausted. The fact was, we were *all* exhausted. It's tough work trying to jump-start a church, and the laypeople involved were just as burned out as I was. As always when a new church is getting underway, there was tension — both creative tension and some that was not so creative.

Cliff walked out of my study and back to the living room, where the meeting was going on. I didn't need to be in the meeting (my wife, Loretta, sat on that committee), so I stayed behind. I couldn't go into the meeting and put on a joyful Christian face when everything I had worked for in the past two years was coming unraveled. I stood alone, in my study, staring into the gloom, feeling depressed and sorry for myself. I broke down and wept.

I felt completely alone. Sure, many people in the church loved and supported me, but I couldn't think of one person in that fellowship who was a close friend. I didn't have one person with whom I could safely, honestly be me, the real me — tears, fears, clay feet and all.

The Loneliness of Leadership

Everyone in leadership will experience loneliness. It comes with the territory. But *must* a leader *remain* lonely? No. We don't have to surrender to loneliness. Loneliness is a curable condition.

In my experience, loneliness comes in two different forms: the *loneliness of leadership* and *social loneliness*. The first kind, the loneliness of leadership, comes to every individual who

- steps out ahead and scouts the trail,
- strides the bridge of the ship,
- occupies the corner office,
- wears the sandals of a prophet, or
- stands in the pulpit.

It's the loneliness that can be fully appreciated only after you've sat behind the sign that reads THE BUCK STOPS HERE.

Sometimes, the loneliness of leadership means I feel the heavy weight of decision making — a weight nobody else can carry for me. Sometimes the loneliness of leadership makes me wonder if somebody painted a bull's eye on my forehead. Sometimes it even gives me a kind of glorious feeling, like, "Gee, here I am, battered and bleeding, sharing the sufferings of Christ; ain't I wonderful?"

But usually, I find that the loneliness of leadership leaves me wondering, "Where did everybody go?" I experienced this feeling in a profound way during my last pastorate. It was a church I had served for fourteen years, and in that church I had many friends — people I count as *close* friends to this day.

Near the end of my ministry there, I began to feel strongly that the only hope for our society, for the worldwide Body of Christ, and for our own local church was for us to experience an awakening, an intervention, a supernatural work of God. I had lost all faith in programs and projects and all the usual things churches do in the name of Christian ministry. We needed something truly extraordinary to take place in the church. Even though I felt this awakening had to be God's work, done in God's own power, I was convinced (and I continue to be convinced) that Christians can do some things to prepare themselves for God's intervention.

So in late 1987, I began to preach my vision of sustained corporate prayer throughout our church, as well as in concert with other churches. I preached on the history of revivals. I talked about the changes that had to be made in individual lives and individual churches before the Spirit of God could move and act. I said one of the preconditions for revival is that we acknowledge our desperate and impoverished state, our powerlessness and our sinfulness, so that we could truly appreciate the magnitude of God's grace and power. Finally, I issued a call for our church to commit itself to an intense level of prayer.

The congregation shrugged.

It was the first time I had felt strong resistance to a series of messages in that church. I had run my God-given vision up the flagpole, and no one saluted. There was no hostility or opposition, but there were no huzzas either. When people hear a joke that falls flat, they laugh politely, but it's clear that no one thinks it's funny. That's how people responded to my vision: politely but without enthusiasm. I sensed many were hoping I would get over this revival thing and get on to something else.

I don't say this to disparage that church. It remains a fine church filled with dedicated Christians, and God is clearly doing a tremendous work there. My point might best be expressed with an analogy:

I was like a trail scout leading a wagon train of settlers across the prairie. I had called out, "Follow me! California's this-a-way!" Then I set off on the westward trail, confident that the settlers would be right at my heels. After the first couple of miles I suddenly realized I was alone. I turned around and there, off in the distance where I left them, were the wagons still huddled inside the walls of Fort Courage. I was hiking the trail by myself.

That's the loneliness of leadership.

The Ups and Downs of Leadership Loneliness

This kind of loneliness has its upside and its downside. Let's take the downside first.

Such loneliness can easily make one feel detached from the people God called you to serve. When I make a decision or take a stand that nobody rallies around, it's easy for me to mutter, "Well, I don't need these people. My loyalty is to the kingdom of God, not to this local church." It's like the feeling Charlie Brown expressed in the *Peanuts* comic strip, "I love mankind. It's people I can't stand." As leaders, we are every bit as self-contradictory as Charlie when we fall into the trap of thinking, *I love the kingdom of God. It's the church I can't stand.*

The upside of this loneliness is that it puts me in touch with my own needs — my need of God, my need of love, my need of other people. After about a half-hour of wallowing in that trough of misery in my study, I sat down at my desk and picked up the phone. I dialed the number of a man who had always been a booster and an encourager to me. He answered on the first ring.

"Dale," I said, "it's Ben. I need to talk to somebody."

He seemed surprised that his pastor would call him with a need. He also seemed pleased that *he* was the one I chose to call. "Sure, Pastor," he said. "Come on over."

I went out by the back door and drove to Dale's house. I arrived feeling broken and a little embarrassed, but when Dale opened the door and shook my hand, I immediately felt the warmth of his welcome. Though I didn't stay long, we had a good honest talk. He listened intently as I groaned about my situation.

That talk with Dale was a gift of God's grace to me. It was the beginning of what has been one of the closest and best friendships of my life.

Loneliness forces me to go deeper with my friendships and deeper with God. When I find myself out on the trail wondering, *Where did everybody go?* it's time to spend some time on my knees and in fellowship with people whose wisdom and caring I genuinely trust. Loneliness forces me to take a reality check: Am I out on the trail all alone because the settlers have lost their nerve or because the trail scout has lost his way?

Social Loneliness

The second kind of loneliness — what I call *social loneliness* — is quite simply the loneliness that comes when you feel you have no close friends, no one to share yourself with and relax with. That's the condition I found myself in during my first pastorate, when I felt my ministry was coming unglued, when elders were abandoning ship. Sure, I had "friends" — people with whom I was more or less "simpatico," people who were cordial and supportive of my ministry. But I didn't have tested-under-fire friends I could count on to be

- safe
- unshockable
- reliable
- honest
- gentle (when needed)
- tough (when called for)

That kind of friend is hard to find. Sometimes you have to seek them out. Sometimes, by the grace of God, they come to you.

I've already mentioned briefly how, early in my present pastorate, two men came to me and said, "Ben, we want to make you an offer, and you can respond to it any way you choose. We want to stand with you and uphold your work. We're ready to pray with you and meet with you. We're ready to roll up our sleeves and get dirt under our fingernails. If there's anything we can do to support you and encourage you, just say the word, and we'll do it."

I was skeptical at first. Over the years, I had heard many similar statements. Sometimes such a speech means, "We want to be in control," or, "We want to be in the inner circle, next to the pastor." So I went slowly in my relationship with these two men.

But as weeks passed, I could see they meant what they said. They never attached any strings to our friendship. They never intruded on my schedule. If I needed help or prayer or someone to talk to, they were there — instantly and completely at my service. They have become my Aaron and Hur, tirelessly holding my arms up through the battle. It has been such a refreshing and encouraging relationship that I will gladly get out of bed early on a Saturday morning just to have breakfast and talk and pray with them. I'll lose sleep to be with these guys, because they are *friends* in the deepest, truest sense of the word.

Furthermore, this experience has shown me that deep friendships have enhanced my pastoral role. Having close emotional ties to a few kindred souls in the church has helped to make the worship experiences, the funerals, the weddings, the births, and baptisms all the more rich and meaningful.

Though some pastors — afraid of appearing to have favorites — try to have a lot of relatively superficial relationships throughout the congregation, I can't. I can't be friends with everybody. I have to have a few close friendships. I can't deny my own humanness, my need for friendships.

Loneliness Barriers

Still, it's not as if we can simply decide to make friends and do it. Some barriers stand between us, as pastors, and the friends we need, barriers that need to be overcome.

Some parishioners, for instance, want to keep us up on a pedestal, as little porcelain icons. They may want to see us up close and personal — that is, they may enjoy having lunch with us, working with us in ministry, or talking theology or C. S. Lewis with us. But many laypeople are not prepared to see us as fallible, vulnerable human beings.

They'll acknowledge our humanity in a general way ("Sure, I know he's not perfect . . ."), but they really cannot handle getting close enough to see that we hurt, we bleed, we experience doubts and fears, we cry, we swear, we argue with our wives, we yell at our kids, we kick the dog. If people actually see us doing the same things under pressure that others do, they think less of us — at least some people do. They think, *Gee, I thought this guy was a servant of God. I guess I was wrong.*

In some sense, we *should* be on a pedestal, for example, when we preach. When we step into the pulpit, we should do so with prophetic, transcendent authority. I've even said from the pulpit, "When I preach, I want you to give me the same attention and respect you would give to Jesus himself, because I believe he wants to say something to you today."

The problem — for me and many of my parishioners — is that it's hard to change hats when I step out of the pulpit. The question becomes, how do I become real and vulnerable outside of the pulpit without undermining my authority inside the pulpit?

In addition, institutional expectations tend to separate me from the people. If I am expected to give the bulk of my time to programs, administration, preaching, and other organizational duties, I don't have much time for friends. Yes, I will spend lots of time with people — meeting with them, planning with them, attending banquets and luncheons with them, teaching them, and preaching to them — but I won't spend much time visiting with them in their homes or counseling with them. I won't have time to simply relax with them and get to know them.

It's amazing the degree to which this holds true in my own life. I live right next door to one of my parishioners — and I never see him except on Sunday! When Jeff shakes my hand on the way out of the sanctuary, we always laugh and say, "See you next Sunday!"

Then there's the busyness perception. Many parishioners I would like to spend time with think I'm too busy to welcome a social invitation. Frankly, I'd make time if I received such invitations, but I don't get many invitations to parties or concerts or quiet, relaxing dinners with friends. I often hear, "I didn't bother to call you because I know you're so busy." People are always amazed when I tell them I'm glad to be invited out.

On the other hand, a few people continually invite you out, try to befriend you, and you know that it is unlikely you will develop a friendship. You don't dislike the person; you simply recognize that, for one reason or another, there is little potential for a deep friendship to ever emerge. This sounds harsh, but it's true. You often find yourself spending social time with people you'd rather not.

It's not cold or unloving not to be someone's best friend. I can still be that person's pastor; I can still seek to shepherd this person in issues of heart and spirit. But I can't be everybody's best friend. That means I will have to turn down invitations for lunch or to play golf from time to time. On one occasion I even had to say to someone, "I can't be your close friend. I care about you, and I want to minister to you, but I can't be your buddy." That was hard, and this individual was clearly hurt. But I know it was the right thing to do.

Internal Blocks

These loneliness barriers above are all *external* barriers. But for many of us, the real cause of our loneliness as leaders lies not without but within, in internal blockages that prevent deep, close friendships.

As we already noted, pastors are prone to busyness. But some of us are driven to lead busier lives than necessary. When we are compulsive about work, it's going to interfere with relationships.

In every true friendship, there is a beautiful, exuberant, almost wanton carelessness about time. Some of the most important "work" that is done when two good friends get together is "killing time." And "killing time" is anathema to the workaholic. When a workaholic gets together with friends, he anxiously rubs his hands together and wants to have an earnest conversation, and usually that means talking shop.

I know a few intense, workaholic pastors who approach friendships with the same compulsive intensity that they approach everything else. They think to themselves, *The big lack in my life is friendships. I must make friends!* So they become "open" and "honest" in a studied, almost posed way. They salt their conversation with a few profane words to show they are being "real." They approach friendship as a task like any other, and the result is that friendships are killed. It would be funny if it wasn't so pathetic.

In a true, close friendship, people have to take time to lighten up, to let go of the need to talk about "important" subjects. Trivialities are important in a friendship. So is silliness. And the most serious business of any friendship is laughter. Frankly, workaholics are bores.

In addition, it's not uncommon for leaders to feel like impostors. We are often called to carry responsibilities far beyond our abilities. Sometimes we feel, *If people really saw me for who I am, I would be seen as a fraud. I'm just passing myself off as spiritual or likable or knowledgeable or capable — and someday the jig is going to be up, and I will be unmasked.* We fear the rejection and the withdrawal of love and friendship that would bring.

The impostor complex causes us to withdraw or withhold

ourselves from others. *No one can accept the real me*, we think, so we project a persona instead.

Another internal block that often leads to loneliness is, ironically, that we are ill at ease with ourselves. We are uncomfortable in our own company. The philosopher Blaise Pascal once observed that the preponderance of human problems comes down to our inability to sit alone in a room.

When we are uncomfortable in our own company, we are unable to have rich, meaningful relationships with other people. If I'm afraid of what I will find whenever I look deep inside myself, then clearly I am going to be terrified of disclosing my deepest self to others. As a result, all my relationships will be superficial at best — and I am doomed to remain lonely. I will be lonely even in the company of my wife, my children, and my friends because the deepest part of me will remain hidden from view.

Finally, we fear betrayal. Once I was leading an important goal-setting meeting involving most of the staff and lay leaders in the church. A close friend of mine thought that some of the ideas I was proposing were completely wrong-headed, and he had told me so in private. Because of our friendship, he wouldn't attack my ideas head-on in the meeting, so instead he dealt them glancing blows. He is blessed (and sometimes cursed) with an agile wit, and he delivered a wisecrack during the meeting that was devastatingly funny.

It really hurt. My friend didn't intend to be cruel, but I felt like a complete idiot nonetheless. Few things are more painful in life than being sabotaged by a close friend.

My nimble-witted pal immediately regretted what he had said, and he has since apologized for it. But I learned it's possible that a good friend and I will find ourselves on opposite sides of an issue in the church.

As we go deeper into relationship with another person, we disclose hidden recesses of ourselves, and we make ourselves vulnerable. Our friend may betray or misunderstand us. Or he or she may become disappointed, or horrified, by who we are.

It is natural to fear rejection and betrayal, but the risks that come with investing in deep relationships are worth taking. If we don't acknowledge and accept those risks, we doom ourselves to loneliness.

Seven Keys to Unlocking Loneliness

Out of my own trial-and-error experience, I've discovered a number of keys to help me find and maintain close friendships. They minimize the risks and deepen the joy of investing in relationships:

● *Take the initiative.* Most of us give little conscious thought and planning to our contacts with others. When I'm feeling alone and friendless, that's a sign I need to give more focused attention to forming new friendships or to renewing existing relationships.

Instead of saying, "We ought to get together sometime," I need to open my planner and say, "When is your next free evening?" Instead of wondering why I never get invited out, I need to call a friend and say, "What are you doing Friday night?" Friendships are too important to leave to chance. They need intentional care and nurture.

● *Seek friends who make few demands.* One sign of a good friend is that he or she doesn't try to get something out of you. Good friends don't clutch at each other; they hold each other lightly. In *The Four Loves*, C.S. Lewis says that friendship is the most free and least binding form of love. I have found that to be true.

After a worship service, church meeting, or potluck usually a number of people flock to me and want to talk. The interesting thing is that my best and closest friends seldom approach me at those moments. They instinctively know not to place additional demands on my time. When I am in my pastoral role, they back off because they know I need to be available to as many people as possible.

● *Seek friends who are fundamentally sound.* I believe it is critically important to seek out friends who are fundamentally sound and comfortable with themselves. These are people with whom I will be taking off my mask; I need to know they have the insight and ego-strength to unmask as well.

This is not to say that we should seek out people who have seemingly few problems. We are all broken people to one degree or another. Yet I have been fortunate to have found a few confidants and intimates who are, in heart and soul, fundamentally healthy, who have the ability (as Pascal said) to sit alone in a room, who have the honesty and strength to enter into a mutual, vulnerable relationship with another human being.

● *Seek friendships with peers.* God often speaks to my wife, Loretta, in the middle of the night. She wakes up, and she has a message for me, and it's uncanny how often that message is exactly what I need to hear.

One morning, I arose early; I dressed and started to walk out of the room. Then I heard my wife's muffled voice from under the covers of the bed: "You need a friend outside the church, someone who is your professional peer."

Later that week, I shared with my men's group what my wife had said. One of the men in the group said, "You know, I've been thinking exactly the same thing for the past two months: 'Ben needs a friend who's a peer outside the church.' And I know just the guy. He's a friend of mine. I'll introduce you." So this fellow set up an introduction with a well-known pastor in New York City.

Over our first lunch together, I told this pastor the chain of events leading to our meeting. "Now, we don't really know each other," I said, "so my feelings won't be hurt if you say no, but . . . would you be my friend?"

He laughed and said, "Yeah, I'll be your friend."

I had never simply asked someone to be my friend before, but on this occasion I believe God wanted it to happen. He and I have gotten together or talked on the phone a number of times since, and we are in the process of becoming good friends.

I believe every leader needs that kind of friendship — a friendship with a peer outside of his own church or organization. Although staff relationships are important, there is more emotional freedom in an outside relationship. Some issues — such as considering a call to another place — are better wrestled with outside of staff relationships.

● *Take time for solitude.* I believe the most potent strategy for punching our way through times of loneliness is to use our solitude as an opportunity to go deeper with God. Ironically, one of the best cures for loneliness is to be alone. Solitude forces me to become more focused on God and his sufficiency. It forces me to face myself, and to learn to become comfortable with myself again.

Loneliness, like any pain in our lives, has a potential for making us better people and better leaders. It puts us in touch with our humanity and brokenness. It sweeps out our hearts and makes us more tender, more attentive to God's Spirit and more sensitive to the needs of others. It's a lot like fasting: just as fasting heightens our awareness and appreciation of food, so loneliness deepens our sense of gratitude for the fellowship of God and others.

A Mystery and a Grace

The machinery of friendship functions in conversation, in laughter, and (much more than we realize) in silence. Many unspoken messages pass between friends. Even when nothing at all is said, volumes of meaning are communicated.

Friendship is a mystery. How do friendships begin? With a chance meeting in a hallway or with a casual introduction on a tennis court or over breakfast with mutual acquaintances. Two people talk. Something clicks. Something indefinable happens. One person says, "Hey, let's get together again." In time, that tenuous connection might dissolve — or it just might ripen into a deep and lifelong friendship.

Genuine friendship doesn't happen often, but when it does it is a delight and a surprise and a grace. It's a quality that can't be captured and frozen in time; it can only be appreciated in motion, like the gracefulness of a dance.

God intervened for Shadrach, Meshach, and Abednego,
but only after they were surrounded by flames.
— *Marshall Shelley*

Epilogue

H arry Truman wasn't the first to suggest that leaders have to
endure heat or else flee the kitchen.

Christian leaders have always had to operate in extreme temperatures — whether the bitter-cold loneliness of living by different standards, the oppressive and sultry heat of impossible
expectations, or the white-hot anger of an incensed critic.

Consider the trio of young leaders in the Book of Daniel who
endured both thermal and emotional heat for their stance on worship, an issue that continues to elevate the temperatures of many

pastors and church leaders today.

Hananiah, Mishael, and Azariah, who had been raised as leaders in their homeland, were uprooted and relocated to serve a different constituency. They accepted the training necessary for their new positions. They even obliged when their names were taken from them and replaced with foreign names. They became administrators in an unfriendly bureaucracy.

But they would not lend their support to a worship service they found repugnant.

When they did not attend the service, they were reported by some apparently jealous rivals. Their case was taken before the king. The heat was on, and even greater heat was threatened. King Nebuchadnezzar told the three, known to us, of course, as Shadrach, Meshach, and Abednego, to bow to his command and worship the image of gold, or else he would sentence them to death by fiery furnace.

They stood before the king and calmly held their ground.

"If we are thrown into the blazing furnace," they replied, "the God we serve is able to save us from it. . . . But even if he does not, we want you to know, O king, that we will not serve your gods or worship the image of gold you have set up."

The king ordered the death sentence carried out.

God did not save them from being tied up, nor did he prevent them from being thrown into the fire. You wonder what the three were thinking as they were hurled into the flames.

But God did intervene, *after* they were surrounded by flames. The fire served only to burn off the ropes that bound them. To the amazement of the king and the onlookers, God not only kept them from being lethally burned, but the Bible says, "There was no smell of fire on them." Somehow they managed to walk away from the ordeal without a lingering odor.

Returning from the world of the fiery furnace to the world of the congregational pressure cooker, I'm impressed that the three authors of this book have also experienced the flames. God has not chosen to grant them immunity from the heat, but he has kept them from lethal burns. And when you're with Leith Anderson, Jack Hayford, and Ben Patterson, you don't smell lingering smoke, either physically or emotionally. They've been in the fire, but they haven't been burned. Their attitudes toward ministry are not scarred and calloused but tender and open.

One final observation: it was in the fire that Shadrach, Meshach, and Abednego experienced the supernatural presence of a fourth man in the fire.

If you are in church leadership, the flames and pressures are probably inevitable. But my prayer, and the prayer of the other authors and editors of this book, is that you, too, may discover God's presence most visibly when you're in the midst of the heat.